J. P. Arendzen

Ten Minutes a Day to Heaven

SOPHIA INSTITUTE PRESS®
Manchester, New Hampshire

Ten Minutes a Day to Heaven is an abridged edition of *Faith and Common Sense: Meditations for Sundays and Holidays* (London: Burns, Oates, and Washbourne Ltd., 1938). This 2002 edition by Sophia Institute Press® contains minor editorial revisions to the original text and doesn't include the preface in the original edition. The chapters have been reordered and grouped according to theme, and some have been combined.

Sophia Institute Press®
Box 5284, Manchester, NH 03108
1-800-888-9344
www.sophiainstitute.com

Nihil obstat: Reginald Phillips, S.Th.L., *Censor Deputatus*
Imprimatur: Leonellus Can. Evans, *Vic. Gen.*
Westminster, September 19, 1938

Library of Congress Cataloging-in-Publication Data

Arendzen, J. P. (John Peter), b. 1873.
  Ten minutes a day to heaven / J. P. Arendzen.
    p. cm.
  Rev. ed. of: Faith and common sense. 1938.
  Includes bibliographical references.
  ISBN 1-928832-75-X (alk. paper)
  1. Christian life — Catholic authors. 2. Catholic Church
    Doctrines. I. Arendzen, J. P. (John Peter), b. 1873. Faith
    and common sense. II. Title.
BX2350.3 .A74 2003
248.4'82 — dc21   2002153924

03 04 05 06 07 08 09 10 9 8 7 6 5 4 3 2 1

Ten Minutes a Day
to Heaven

Contents

Part Two: *Cultivate your spiritual life*

Part Three: *Live your Faith*

Part Four: *Practice virtue*

Part Five: *Fight sin*

Foreword

At times it's easy to think that your journey to Heaven calls for more time, virtue, and courage than you have to give. The demands of family, work, and everyday life may leave you little time even to pray, much less to grow in virtue and in your understanding of the Faith.

But it's precisely within the context of your everyday life, with all its demands, that God calls you to grow in holiness. What you must learn to do, therefore, is to use each moment and circumstance of your daily life to advance on the road to Heaven.

That's where this book can help you. In brief chapters that take only minutes to read, Fr. J. P. Arendzen teaches you how to put God first in your life, to pray better, to become holier, to fight sin, to practice charity toward others — in short, to advance on the road to Heaven. Take just ten minutes each day to read one chapter and to put into practice what it teaches, and that small daily investment will bring you an everlasting reward: Heaven.

*Ten Minutes a Day
to Heaven*

Editor's note: The biblical quotations in the following pages are taken from the Douay-Rheims edition of the Old and New Testaments. Where applicable, quotations have been cross-referenced with the differing names and enumeration in the Revised Standard Version, using the following symbol: (RSV =).

Part One

Center your
life on God

⌒

Chapter One

Commend your journey
to Heaven to God's care

Not infrequently you come across loud and ludicrous advertise-ments of self-styled geniuses who will teach you, for a modest fee, by word of mouth or by correspondence, how to have confidence in yourself or how to overcome that fatal shyness, that feeling of impotence and inferiority which hampers all your undertakings and prevents success. They will teach you self-reliance, boldness in speech and behavior, and daring in enterprise. They will tell you to secure by your own unaided efforts a radiant future. All for a small fee — booklet included!

In worldly affairs, there may possibly be something in it, about one percent of what is claimed, but in the great business of going to Heaven, the key to success is reliance on the grace of God and utter distrust in ourselves. The source of endless failures, and the reason for even final disaster of passably good people is too much self-reliance apart from God. People forget Original Sin. Original Sin has weakened and wounded our nature.

Our nature is not fundamentally corrupted; that is quite true. We still have free will. We have many good instincts. We often dream of heroic deeds — like St. Peter a few hours before his fall.[1] He was prepared to go to prison and death for his Master, but as a matter of fact he did not, except some thirty years later, when he had learned more dependence on God.

The man who, on seeing the sins of others, lays his hand on his breast and proudly says, "Now, I could never do that!" is like the apostle who boldly looked around the company of his fellow apostles and then said to his Master: "Although all should be scandalized in Thee, yet not I."[2] There are and have been many fairweather saints who, when the sun was shining, sang a boastful song of their future prowess, but who, on the first blast of the storm, lay prostrate in the mire of sin. It is strange that we learn so little by experience.

There is not one of us who could not tell a tale of grand plans and poor execution, of great promises and little fulfillment, of big words and small things to show for them, a rattling of swords before the foe was in sight and a precipitate flight when he appeared. And if we examined ourselves, we would see that in all cases it was due to overwhelming self-confidence. On the occasions when, by God's grace, we really triumphed, our triumph followed humble anxiety, lest we should fail.

There is an old story of the Scotsman who told the overconfident young preacher who had gone to the pulpit with a swagger, but left it crestfallen after a hopeless breakdown, "Man, if you had gone up such as you came down, you would have come down such as you went up."

Must, then, the Christian be forever a craven and a coward and be whimpering and whining about his weakness and incapacity? Must he be a chronic sufferer from an inferiority complex? Must he never feel any pluck or courage and face the future like a man? No, indeed. But his confidence is through Christ in God.

[1] Cf. Matt. 26:35.
[2] Mark 14:29.

A Christian grasps his crucifix and repeats with St. Paul, "I can do all things in Him who strengtheneth me!"[3] Of myself, I may be nothing, but with Christ I'll face principalities and powers and spirits of wickedness in high places. With Christ even the weakness of my human nature is filled with indomitable strength. Without Christ I can do nothing, but He can make divine force flow from His manhood into mine and transform me into a hero if He chooses.

I have unlimited strength at my disposal, if only I pray. I must acknowledge that of myself I am feeble and worthless; that, left to myself, the most paltry temptation could overthrow me, and then I must look up to Christ and say, "Thou art all, and there is nothing created that can resist Thy might. With Thee nothing is impossible, not even to strengthen this feeble creature who depends utterly on Thee, and so to strengthen this creature that all must yield to the power borrowed from Thee."

Let any man look around in the history of mankind, and he will not fail to see that the saints have performed feats of superhuman strength, that they have endured beyond what human nature by itself can bear, that their willpower has been the amazement of their fellowmen, that their perseverance has been the marvel of their own generation, that their achievements have exceeded that of scores of others who tried to blunder through by themselves. Then let him ask himself, "What was their secret?" They will with one voice answer him: "Our confidence was with Christ in God. It was God who worked in us, and strength was made perfect in infirmity."[4]

---

[3] Phil. 4:13.
[4] Cf. 2 Cor. 12:9.

☞

Chapter Two

Recognize who God is
and who you are

The distance in dignity between creatures can be immense, as the difference between a clod of earth and the mind of man, but no distance is so vast as that between God and His creature. The faintest glow of the wick of a candle compared with the blazing brilliancy of the noonday sun in an open sky is still greater than man compared with his God. The tiniest drop of water as compared with the ocean is still bigger than the mightiest created spirit compared with Him who made it. We may not know the precise number of drops it takes to fill the ocean; we know it is limited and can be numbered, but no adding up of creatures, however beautiful and mighty, would ever equal God.

God is beyond and above, all-surpassing and all-transcending, and there is no common measure between Him and us. We are His image and likeness indeed, but it is only a reflection, an analogy; the reality exceeds the image by the infinite totality of its being.

The Blessed Trinity brings us face-to-face with the mysteriousness of God. The very unveiling of the inner life of God in the eternal coexistence of Father, Son, and Holy Spirit deepens our sense of mystery and awe. The beginningless origin of the Son from the bosom of the Father, the coming forth of the Third Person as the subsisting love between Them both, is to our mind, although revealed, still the profoundest of secrets, and it brings home to us the littleness of our human minds and the tiny strength of our understanding.

It makes us feel our need of adoration and teaches us mental lowliness. Adoration is the highest form of prayer.

The simplest and most spontaneous form of prayer is, no doubt, that of petition. Ask and you shall receive.[5] In our poverty and distress, in our many wants and desires, in ill-health and ill-repute, among all the dangers of life, we instinctively turn to God and come as suppliants before His throne, for He is good and mighty and can help us in our needs. This prayer of petition is indeed good in itself and pleasing to God, both meritorious and efficacious and, while we are here below, never to be omitted, yet it is but the first and not the highest form of prayer.

Moreover, as long as we are sinners, we need the prayer of penitence and propitiation. In a way, it is only a kind of prayer of petition, since it is a begging for pity and pardon arising from the consciousness of our guilt.

Next comes the prayer of thanksgiving when, filled with gratitude, we praise God, for He has shown Himself so good to us. But highest of all is adoration, the worship of God for what He is in Himself, the bending of our knees in sheer homage to the divine majesty and the proclaiming of His everlasting glory.

In this kind of prayer, we join the cherubim and seraphim, who cry out without ceasing, "Holy, holy, holy, Lord God of hosts. Heaven and earth are full of Thy glory."[6] Prayer of petition and propitiation will pass away — in Heaven there will be a place for it no longer — but praise and adoration will remain throughout

---

[5] Cf. Matt 7:7.

[6] Cf. Isa. 6:3.

eternity. The mystery of the Blessed Trinity, because it deals with God as He is in Himself, leads us on to this sublime kind of prayer of awestruck reverence for the living God, who is Father, Son, and Holy Spirit.

We adore Thee, O Father,
Source of the Godhead,
who of Thyself dost possess the divinity.
None gave it to Thee, but Thou hast it
to give it to Thy Son before all ages,
Thy only-begotten One,
Thy image, the splendor of Thy glory.

We adore Thee, Son of God, God of God,
light of light, true God of true God,
of the same substance as Thy Father,
by whom all things are made.

We adore Thee, Holy Spirit,
proceeding from the Father and the Son,
Thou Lord and Giver of life,
Thou eternal self-subsisting Love of God.

Through the lightsome cloud of faith,
we see Thee, O God: three in persons
yet one in nature, glory, and divinity.
We sing Thy praises as yet with mortal lips
for what Thou art, and we hope to praise Thee
in company with all the heavenly host
when at last we shall see Thee
without mystery in majesty unveiled.

As contemplating the Trinity rouses us to adoration, so it fills us with intellectual humility. Our mental pride is humbled before the mystery that surpasses our understanding; we confess that there is a great deal in Heaven and earth that is not dreamed of in our philosophy. Man's first sin was one of intellectual pride. The serpent promised that man should know as much as God, and that God's commandment was only a trick to prevent man from becoming all-wise, as God Himself. In stark folly, man believed the deceiver, and all he got to know was that he was helpless and naked.

But it takes man a long time to learn humility. The moment he obtains some fresh piece of knowledge concerning the laws of God's creation, he begins to be puffed up and fancies himself nearing omniscience. He mocks at mystery and is ready to solve all problems.

Tell him he must believe, without knowing the how and the why, and he scoffs at the thought. Ask him to accept a thing as a fact, because God said so, even though he knows not the why and wherefore, he will reject it as useless mystification in his annoyance, in his baffled vanity that he cannot see around it and through it. So there are many to whom the mystery of the Blessed Trinity is a stumbling block and a stone of offense, instead of an act of gracious, tender condescension of God to man in letting him know even faintly and by faith what passes in that boundless sea of endless life of the divine nature in a Trinity of Persons.

We, who were baptized in the name of the Father, the Son, and the Holy Spirit, should lovingly bend our neck under the sweet yoke of faith, finding pleasure in humbling ourselves before infinite truth, paying willing homage to boundless wisdom. Prostrate in our littleness before divine greatness, we should repeat the words of Scripture: "Oh, the depth of the riches of the wisdom and the knowledge of God! How incomprehensible are His judgments, how unsearchable His ways! Of Him and by Him and in Him are all things. To Him be glory forever. Amen."[7]

----

[7] Rom. 11:33, 36.

Chapter Three

Understand the greatness
God has bestowed on you

After the Trinity and the Incarnation, no mystery of our Catholic Faith is greater than that of our supernatural state: the miracle of sanctifying grace and the indwelling of God in our soul.

Unfortunately, the majority of our fellowmen have not the remotest idea what *supernatural* really means. Many imagine that it means no more than spiritual as opposed to material, human as opposed to animal. Anything unwonted they forthwith dub "supernatural," having but the vaguest notion of what they mean by the word.

We know that the bestowal of sanctifying grace is the most astounding marvel in all the universe, for it raises us, created though we be, to a height of dignity that surpasses all created things. St. Peter describes it as a sharing in, a participation in, the divine nature.[8] St. Paul again and again describes it as a new creation.[9]

Our blessed Lord Himself speaks of it as a new birth and, in speaking to Nicodemus, insists that the entrance on earth into the

[8] 2 Pet. 1:4.
[9] Cf. 2 Cor. 5:17; Gal. 6:15.

kingdom of Heaven consists in being born again.[10] Many take this in a vague sort of way: the sinner stops sinning and begins a decent, respectable conduct and thus, in some sense, starts a new life. God forgives the past, in the sense that He lets bygones be bygones, and lets the sinner off his punishment, and allows him to make a fresh start, just as among men, sometimes a kind-hearted soul will overlook the past of some wild youth and give him another chance "to make good," as the saying goes.

Of the wonder of the "new creation," "the new birth," and "the sharing in the divine nature," such people know nothing. They do not understand that sanctifying grace is a physical reality produced in the human soul by the creative omnipotence of God — a spiritual quality and state to which no created being, whether angel or man, has any right, and which no created being could obtain for himself even after millions of years of labor and striving. They do not grasp that it is a spiritual gift infused into the soul by the power and goodness of Almighty God, really and truly a new life, which makes us akin to God and by which we become His adopted children.

This divine adoption is not just an exaggerated metaphor, a kind of divine pretense; it is a sober fact, based on some tremendous change wrought in our innermost being, the essence of our soul. The infinite Creator deigns again to exercise His unique privilege as Creator. He deigns to say, "Let there be light," and there is light, a light far exceeding that of sun or moon in our firmament. The raising of one little child in Baptism, or of one sinner by absolution to the state of grace, is a greater work of God than the production of the whole material universe out of nothing.

One single soul in the state of grace is worth more than a thousand worlds whose colossal bulk revolves through space, for that soul lives by an ineffable sharing in the life of God Himself. Father,

[10] John 3:5.

14

Son, and Holy Spirit dwell within it, pervade it, and hold it as fire holds the object that glows within it. That soul is destined, after a short stay on earth in its mortal body, to see God face-to-face, to know God and love God after the fashion in which God knows and loves Himself, to possess God directly without any go-between, as a friend embraces a friend, as a lover enjoys his beloved.

Now, sanctifying grace on earth is the same thing as glory is in Heaven: grace is the seed, glory is the fruit, but seed and fruit are only the same life continued through growth into maturity. St. Leo the First[11] said well, "O Christian, acknowledge thy own greatness." Let our soul magnify the Lord and our spirit exult in God, our Savior, for He that is mighty has done great things in us.[12]

---

[11] St. Leo the Great (d. 461), Pope from 440 and Doctor.
[12] Cf. Luke 1:46-47, 49.

Chapter Four

⌒

Revere the name of Jesus

"What is there in a name?" asks a scornful proverb, and of the present names of men, we might well say that it is an idle question. Our present names are but arbitrary series of sounds without meaning, which chance to be associated with some person.

It is not so with the name of Jesus. It is the name God chose for Himself, so that He might be designated thereby among the children of men when He had designed to take their nature and dwell among them. It is an adorable name, for it is the name of God the Son, and at that name, "every knee should bow, of those that are in Heaven, on earth, and under the earth, and every tongue should confess that the Lord Jesus Christ is in the glory of God the Father."[13] At that name, all the angels above and all the saints with all the blessed dead who are awaiting their admission into Heaven stand in awe; even the demons in the netherworld must tremble, and we on earth in deepest reverence bow our heads and adore. It is the name of God.

For God, as God, in His infinite divine nature, we men could never have found a name, for among us names are used for finite,

---

[13] Phil. 2:10-11.

17

limited, circumscribed individual creatures to distinguish them from their fellows. God needs no distinguishing from others. He is not just one among many. He has no compeers. There is no need to single Him out among a crowd. In divine loveliness, He is above all created multiplicity. He transcends all that is manifold in the divine unity of His nature.

We could never have named Him as we name one of our equals. We could only use one ray of His infinite glory, use it as a description, imperfect and feeble and as a token for His endless majesty. Until Christ came, God did not deign to assume a proper name. In answer to Moses, who asked His name, He answered only, "I am who I am. He who is, that is my name."[14] His eternal, boundless Being must stand for a name. But in the fullness of time, God condescended to our ways and gave Himself a proper name. Hence, at the hearing of the name of Jesus, the first thought of every Christian is that of adoration, a sinking down in humility before his Creator, who had deigned to take a creaturely name, even though He sits enthroned above the cherubim, beyond the compass of our finite minds.

With this act of adoration is forthwith mingled a sense of loving intimacy, for Jesus is a human name like our own. We know He is Jesus of Nazareth, the little village of Galilee. It is the name that His mother called Him when He was the baby Jesus of Bethlehem. By that very name we know that He has become like us in all things except in sin.

Although God, He is also truly human. He became one among many. He entered the great human family and did not disdain to be our Brother. By rights we should call Him Master and Majesty, Lord, Sovereign, and King, but we may now greatly dare and call Him Jesus, His proper name. Many a fellow being might be very angry with us if we presumed to call them by their proper name; we

[14] Cf. Exod. 3:14.

must give them their title and status. But our Lord will not be wrathful if in prayer we whisper His name in token of our affection and intimacy with Him.

In public we will not with all-too-easy frequency use that holy name; we will not use it loudly or irreverently among the crowd. But we will use it when He and we are together, as Christians may who know that the Word has become flesh and dwells among us. His name shall be as honey on our lips, as a melody to our ears, as a flame of love in our hearts. We shall use it in holy audacity when His Heart throbs against ours in Holy Communion. Casual, careless, or profane use would be a horror to us and a blasphemy, for blessed is the name of Jesus, true God and true man, but to repeat it in tender devotion is a privilege allowed to those who love Him. It is like our kiss of the sacred wounds when we are alone with our crucifix.

But lastly, we not only know that the name is His, but we also know what it means. God's chosen name is not meaningless, for He is God our Savior and He wishes so to be called, for He redeems His people from their sins.[15] So said the angel to St. Joseph; so said St. Gabriel to Mary, His Virgin Mother.

Every time that name comes to our lips, it is a cry of gratitude for our redemption; it is a cry of supplication for help in danger, for final deliverance from our sins. It is the true name of "the Lamb of God that taketh away the sins of the world,"[16] the name of Him who bore our iniquities and was bruised for our sins.[17] There is no other name in Heaven or on earth by which we can be saved.[18] He bought us pardon at the price of His Blood;[19] He saved us from

---

[15] The name *Jesus* means "God saves."

[16] Cf. John 1:29.

[17] Cf. Isa. 53:5.

[18] Acts 4:12.

[19] 1 Pet. 1:18-19.

death and Hell. Such thoughts flood our mind whenever we hear the sound of that name.

In all danger, by a divine instinct, the Christian utters that name to find safety and to overcome the powers of evil. May all of us praise and glorify that name when we join the multitude of the redeemed who stand around His throne.

Chapter Five

⌒

Preserve God's gift of sanctifying grace

In the Gospel parable of the wedding banquet, the punishment inflicted on the man who did not have on a wedding garment might
seem excessive: "Bind his hands and his feet, and cast him into the
exterior darkness; there shall be weeping and gnashing of teeth."[20]
But the rigor of the punishment is understood as soon as we realize
that the garment in the parable is the symbol of sanctifying grace.
To die without sanctifying grace is to be forever deprived of liberty,
light, and joy.

Bound hand and foot is the one who has lost the liberty of the
children of God and who will be forever the slave of sin and the
bondsman of the Devil. You shall know the truth, our Lord promised to those who followed Him; you shall know the truth, and the
truth shall make you free.[21] The damned have willfully darkened
their minds; they labor under self-inflicted blindness, and hence,
they have forfeited their freedom. Their feet are roped with the
rope of their passions, and they can move only as far as their evil
inclinations will let them. They are like dogs chained to Satan's

[20] Matt. 22:13.
[21] John 8:32.

kennel; they can only fret and fume in the narrow circle around the stake of their own selfishness, where their chain is fastened. Their hands are cuffed together in sign of their utter helplessness of ever doing any good, of ever achieving any useful aim, condemned as they are to never-ending impotence, however great their rage of fruitless striving. Their fingers will always feverishly fumble at the desperate knot they themselves have tied, yet never undo it; their nails will always scratch at the lock they themselves have forged, yet they will never unlock it.

Having refused God's gift of heavenly freedom, they have given themselves into bondage to Satan, who does not loosen his captives, but cruelly tightens the cords of their abject slavery.

"Cast him into exterior darkness": an outcast from the realm of light, a self-willed exile from the land of glory. One cry of mercy, one thought of repentance before death, might have saved him, but he hardened his soul in evil until the last, and now the ministers of God's wrath have flung him out as one flings out a foul beast from the dwelling of the clean, for the sight of his corruption is offensive to the sight of the healthy and the pure.

His is no place in the home of divine splendor and beauty. There is no place for him in the sun; let him sprawl in the darkness, where loathsome things belong. Let murky fog be his covering and black slime be his bed. Let the morn never dawn over his abode and deep night hide his deformities. Let it be the outer darkness far away!

Far away on the outskirts of creation, there must be a chasm between him and the children of the light, as the abyss that was between Dives and Lazarus, a cleft that no one can cross.[22] It must be far away, so that the sound of the wicked may not trouble the just, and that the fragrance of God's Paradise may not be wafted across to the pool of the damned and their bottomless pit. He was one of

[22] Luke 16:26.

those who, while on earth, loved darkness more than the light; he deliberately shielded his eyes against Christ, the Light of the World, and sought the somber paths that lead to the caves of sin. He has fixed his lot; he must live in the underworld, where no ray of God's white majesty pierces, and where no breath is felt of the upper air of Heaven. There shall be weeping and gnashing of teeth.

Tears are sometimes a relief to the mourner, but there are other tears, burning, scalding tears, tears of bitterness and anger, tears of despair, tears that aggravate rather than lessen pain: such will be the tears of the lost.

"Oh, how great is the fire of sin, yet the water of a few tears will put it out," so said St. John Chrysostom fifteen hundred years ago.[23] But he spoke of the tears of repentance shed by the sinner before leaving this earth. It is different with the tears of the impenitent shed after death. They are useless and hopeless and quench no fire of remorse and no fire of the wrath of God. Rather, they sting the eyes that shed them; they make the flames of fire seem fiercer than before. Hence, the wicked weepers grind and gnash their teeth in idle fury against themselves.

They might so easily have been clad in the wedding garment of sanctifying grace, when the King came to see His guests. The garment was offered them, nay, they had even worn it, but then torn it to shreds by their sin, and when the fatal visit came, they were without it and faced the merciful King with obstinate silence, only to change that silence into the sound of ceaseless mourning in the land whence no one returns.

---

[23] St. John Chrysostom (c. 347-407), Archbishop of Constantinople and Doctor; named Chrysostom, or "Golden Mouth" for his eloquent preaching.

Chapter Six

Respond promptly to the graces
God gives you each day

"Waste not, want not" is a homely and useful proverb, but it is more often applied to material goods than spiritual ones, more to things that perish than to things of eternal value.

St. Paul warns us against wasting the most precious thing on earth: divine grace. "We beseech you that you receive not the grace of God in vain."[24] But in many, the waste of grace is appalling. In vain are the offers of divine gifts, in vain the solicitations of God's love, in vain the riches of Christ's Redemption, set before us only for the taking. What is the reason for this squandering of God's generous wealth? It is that miserable word: *tomorrow!* It is that feeble smile with which we say to ourselves, "The day, the week, the month is young yet. I shall do it later on!"

The present writer as a boy used to pass an inn on whose sign stood boldly written, "Free wine tomorrow." This puzzled him much, until even on his childish mind it dawned that it was always tomorrow and never today, since he never saw the expected crowd of cheerful partakers of the innkeeper's generosity. Our dealings

---

[24] Cf. 2 Cor. 6:1.

with God are both similar and yet the reverse. It is God who, in the inn of holy Church, offers the free wine of His divine grace every day, but the glad, careless crowd passes by unheeding, while some, who take notice indeed, answer the call by a condescending and most indifferent "Tomorrow."

St. Paul pleads with us, saying, "Now is the acceptable time; behold now is the day of salvation."[25] If from moment to moment, from day to day, we acted on the graces held out to us, how rich in holiness would we become! Even if we were quick and responsive to every call of grace the instant it came, what treasures would we lay up for ourselves! We should remember: a grace lost may never return. No doubt God often repeats the offer, but He does not always do so. We may give God a casual "Tomorrow," but there may be no invitation for tomorrow; we have reckoned without our host. The grace of God is not a mechanical contrivance that can be drawn upon at will, left unused one day and turned on the next. Every grace is a personal gift from the free love of God.

It is dangerous to play with divine generosity, for God's bounty is not fond foolishness. God is a great lover, who loves to send presents to the soul He loves. If, however, these gifts are, with cool politeness, steadily returned with the remark "Not today, thank you," we must not wonder why, in the end, He stops sending them. Moreover, we should remember that, should He stop sending them, we are in utmost peril of falling into mortal sin.

We may be at the time in the state of grace, and our refusal or postponed acceptance, if you like to call it so, may not be in itself a grievous sin, but we are gradually growing weaker. We become like people in frail health, not possessing any reserve strength. We become like foolish people who live on the very edge of their income. We become like foolhardy jesters balancing on a tightrope with a drop of a hundred feet below.

[25] 2 Cor. 6:2.

Difficult circumstances may surprise us, sore temptations sud-denly befall us, when only a miracle of grace can save us, but what right have we to demand extraordinary graces when with strange impertinence we have long refused lesser ones?

Let us thirdly remember that even if God has pity on us in the hour of dire need and saves us by a miracle of grace, still, dur-ing the period of our negligence, innumerable graces have been wasted; we have not been laying up treasures for eternity. Our state and degree in Heaven depend on our riches at the moment of our death, and we have only our few years here on earth to gather merit for Heaven. Our swift day here below quickly passes, and then the night comes, in which no one can work.[26]

Graces once lost are very difficult to retrieve. In one sense, we might say they are irretrievable, since our span of life is limited and time gone leaves less time to labor for God and our soul. Grace is, as it were, capital to trade with, and the greater the sum in hand, the greater our opportunity for increasing our spiritual endow-ment. Every grace refused or postponed is therefore truly a dead loss that impoverishes the poor, negligent, slovenly soul.

So listen to the call of God here and now. Some act of mortifi-cation, some self-sacrifice, some deed of worship and piety, some generosity to the poor, some word and gesture of kindness to our fellows, some greater care in our prayers and reception of sacra-ments: let us respond to God's grace and be thrifty with God's gifts so that we may acquire riches that never perish.

---

[26] Cf. John 9:4.

Chapter Seven

⌒

Do God's will as He reveals it to you

"I do not want to see the distant scene. One step enough for me." So sang Cardinal Newman in his famous hymn, "Lead, Kindly Light." In these words, we might describe the life of St. Joseph.

A just but silent man was he, of whom not a word is on record, a man entrusted with a most amazing, most difficult task, in which mere human prudence without divine guidance would have been of little avail. "One step enough for me!" Betrothed to our Lady, he was faced with a cruel dilemma before he knew the mystery of the Incarnation, but the moment he knows God's will, he did it and took Mary as his spouse. Faced with strange happenings — angels singing in the sky and shepherds summoned by divine command to worship Mary's Child — he still obeyed the Jewish Law and brought Mother and Child to the Temple and offered his turtledoves to ransom the Babe, for such was the divine command which has not yet been revoked.[27]

When the Magi came and said that King Herod himself intended to follow to worship the Child, it must have seemed strange to him, but he stirred not from his place and slept in peace

[27] Luke 2:22-24.

until the angel's message came: "Take the Child and His Mother, and flee into Egypt."[28] Then forthwith he went with them into the land of exile. There he stayed until the angel came again, telling him to go back to Galilee. Then forthwith he went and dwelled at Nazareth.

The Jewish feasts at Jerusalem he observed, for such was his duty as Jew and son of David, and he took his divine Foster-son with him, for such seemed his duty, since Moses' Law was God's will still. When he lost the Holy Child and found Him again in the Temple, he let Mary speak for him, while he remained silent. He just followed God's will and said nothing.[29] In Nazareth he received the obedience of his Foster-child, while he taught Him the carpenter's trade, for such was clearly the task then set before him.

Our Lady told him the promise that her Son was to sit on the throne of David and rule over the house of Jacob forever. St. Joseph cannot have but expected great and marvelous things in the future, since he knew himself as guardian and foster-father of the Messiah, the promised King and Redeemer. He had heard Simeon praise Him as the light of the Gentiles and the glory of his people Israel.[30] Jesus was now a grown man, yet nothing unusual had happened in the carpenter's shop at Nazareth.

Joseph felt old age creeping in and death approaching, but he peacefully drew his last breath in the arms of Jesus and Mary. He never saw the distant scene: one-step enough for him! The disciples of John the Baptist, over-eager in human, although noble, impatience, would come and ask of Jesus, "Art Thou He who is to come, or do we expect another?"[31] But St. Joseph closed his eyes in death, content that here on earth he did not see the revelation of

[28] Cf. Matt. 2:13.
[29] Luke 2:41-49.
[30] Luke 2:32.
[31] Matt. 11:3.

the glory of the Messianic kingdom. He left the future in God's hands, happy that he himself could fulfill God's will in the present from day to day with hatchets, planes, and saws, with screws, nails, and hammers, shaping and fixing the wood, as a little village carpenter does to gain the livelihood of those dependent on him.

Thus St. Joseph has become the great example for the great number of men to whom it is not given to see distant vistas of glory, but who have to go on step by step through life, seeing God's will clearly only day by day.

Blessed are they who in perfect calm know how to wait on God and make no futile attempts at forestalling divine providence. Do from hour to hour what your hand finds to do, and do it with all your might. Do it because God here and now wills it, and you will be a just man. Drudgery, you say? Perhaps so, and at the same time the finest, noblest thing a man can do.

But should not a man have ideals and visions, and aim high, and hope for great things? Yes, but he should not worry about them. Worrying is not a Christian virtue. Let us be energetic indeed, and within reason even plan for the future, and provide for emergencies, and then resign ourselves to God's will, anxious to do it as soon as we know it.

Then, as St. Joseph, we shall die without bitter regrets and pass away in the arms of Jesus and Mary.

Chapter Eight

⌒

Be faithful in little things

Life consists of trifles. That, at least, is the phrase often heard and on the lips of many. It contains much truth. Human life indeed, considered in its completeness, is great; it is the greatest thing on earth, even if it be the so-called humdrum existence of the undistinguished average man.

All human life is a grand epic of doing God's will, of fighting evil inclinations and, by final triumph, gaining everlasting happiness in Heaven. Yet life consists of trifles. "Because thou hast been faithful in little things, I shall put thee over great ones"[32] will be for all of us, we hope, the verdict of the Great Judge.

These "little things" may be little and momentary acts of self-conquest and resistance to temptation. They may be little acts of piety that, if repeated and continued, coalesce into noble and exalted homage to God. They may be little acts of kindness to our neighbor, by which we fulfill the precept of loving our neighbor as ourselves.

Let us take the bearing of the proverb that life consists of trifles in this third sense. "Greater love no one hath than he who giveth

---

[32] Cf. Matt. 25:21.

his life for his friend."[33] This willingness to give one's life is certainly most convincingly proven if one submits the neck to the sword of a foe in order to save the life of a friend, but a less spectacular surrender of life may in itself be as great, and this may be done by a long series of trifles, lasting perhaps many years.

There is, perhaps, in our domestic circle some person who may be courteously described as a difficult character. At heart such a person may be thoroughly good, but there are some asperities and angularities about his or her conduct that make the life of those around him or her a veritable martyrdom. It may be a trifle to bear with each single outbreak of such unlovable peculiarities, but it is no trifle to pass over with a smile a thousand unpleasantnesses. It is heroism.

The life of a Christian may be one of heroism in a long series of such trifles. There may be in our home someone suffering from an infirmity, hard on those who have to tend to the sick, some chronic invalid who needs almost incessant attention. An hour's nursing may be a trifle, even a day's care may still be a trivial matter, but months and years of it mean the life of a hero.

Perhaps our employment, the way in which we have to make our living, is exacting and troublesome. There may be ten thousand annoyances and small hardships in it, each of which might be considered a trifle, yet greatly to be admired is the man who smilingly passes them over for God's sake. I do say *for God's sake!*

There are people who are cheery by nature, optimists by constitution, to whom it costs little or nothing to be always bright; there are other people who keep a smiling face in business because they think it is good policy, since they cannot afford to quarrel. Superficial cheerfulness may thus be nature or prudence, but when trifles are well borne for God's sake, although they smart and sting, we have the making of a saint.

[33] Cf. John 15:13.

Life is made up of trifles. Which married couple would not assent to this truth? Husband and wife may on the whole be well matched, but there always remain some oddities in which they differ from one another. Trifling, perhaps, such differences are, but their very smallness, or if you choose to say so, their meanness, can be very galling and bitter.

Happy is the man or woman who keeps a sense of proportion and who, overcoming the first feeling of resentment, realizes that they are only trifles and must not, by brooding over them, be magnified into monstrous misdeeds. A pinprick is not a deadly sword thrust, nor is a molehill a mountain, although to angry eyes it may sometimes seem so. How attractive is a person who is perpetually out to do little acts of kindness both at home and outside, a person who is not only considerate, so as to avoid giving even a tiny offense or causing a trifling inconvenience, but who actually seeks for an opportunity to do a small service, to say an extra cheery word, who contrives a smile, when he himself does not quite feel like it, but when he guesses that his smile may bring a little sunshine to somebody else.

No doubt all these things are trifles, but life consists of such trifles. Trifles can make life a hell on earth, and trifles can make it a paradise. There are people who excuse themselves for neglecting trifles by saying that they always look after the big things. But it is no excuse. This accumulation of small things is a big thing. Moreover, those who boast of looking only after big things are usually wrong in estimating the size of things. Many a time, their small thing is a very big one in the eyes of God and man.

"Look after the pence, and the pounds will look after themselves" is a homely proverb that applies even to spiritual things.

Chapter Nine

⤍

Use the gifts and talents God has given you

St. Paul lays stress on the diversity of gifts that it pleases God to bestow on different individuals. The apostle had realized by his own insight and experience of human nature the common failing of mankind: to claim gifts that are not ours. We may possess some undoubted and most conspicuous abilities in one direction, but, strange to say, we are not satisfied; we make little of them, whereas we preen ourselves on others that we scarcely possess or obviously lack.

We are like the crow that would boast of the beauty of its voice or the nightingale of the brilliancy of its plumage. There are people who play the piano exceedingly well, who have in fact a talent for music, but who want to shine in painting, although their dreary daubs prove that they have not the slightest sense of color. There are people who have a really beautiful voice, but whose great anxiety is to show off in athletics, for which they lack all ability. Again and again we hear this justified criticism: if only he would be satisfied with the great powers he possesses, and limit himself to what he knows and can do so well, he would be an outstanding success, but he fritters himself away on things for which he has not the least aptitude.

As it is in the natural sphere, so it is in the supernatural, and St. Paul had unfortunately begun to experience it among his converts at Corinth. God gave diverse privileges to the early Christians — the gifts of prophecy, of languages, of spiritual insight, and so forth — but envy and disorder had crept in among the recipients of these heavenly bestowed powers, and St. Paul had to write that everyone had to be satisfied with his own gifts and functions and not covet his neighbor's.

Human nature has not changed much since St. Paul's day. Every director of souls, every parish priest knows it. To rest content in the little niche in which God has placed us is a splendid virtue, but oh, so rare! So many good and excellent people spoil much of the good work they do, and thwart and hinder their own progress in the spiritual life, because they insist on wanting to do what is evidently not the thing they are apt for, the thing that suits their character and attainments, the thing that God has clearly destined for them. They look at their neighbor who has some other gift, task, and duty, and they imagine they will never be happy until they take his place. As a parish priest once put it: the person who would be a treasure in the choir wants to be in the sacristy, and the man who is needed in the sanctuary thinks that his proper place is at the door of the church. The work that the laity do for the Church is worthy of all admiration and praise, but sometimes part of it is marred and rendered ineffective by little jealousies and the petty encroachments of one worker on the task of another.

This distressing fault may invade, not merely work done for the Church, but even the whole intimate life of the soul. "Now, if I were only placed like Mr. or Mrs. So-and-so, I would make giant strides forward; I might become a saint. But situated as I am, I see no chance. As long as I am in my present position, I can make no headway. If I had the opportunities and the gifts that So-and-so has, I would use them better, perhaps, than he or she, but as it is, it is, with my peculiar temperament, my poor endowments, and the way I am placed, nothing can be done until a change comes."

And thus, time is lost in a strange hankering after some alterations, in a disregarding of our own gifts to long for someone else's, in idle speculation on what we would do if we were different from what we are. To the angels in Heaven, men must resemble a crowd of children at a party where each child is sulking because he has not the toys of another. Those who have had charge of such parties know quite well that however careful the distribution of prizes and presents, there will always be some unpleasant children moping in a corner because he does not have what he wants.

The saints became saints because they acted otherwise. They found themselves as they were and as God made them, lost no time in grumbling or dreaming about if only they were somebody else, but forthwith set to work with the gifts they had, trafficked with their talents, even if they had only two instead of five, and received the divine blessing: Well done, faithful servant, because thou hast been faithful in little things![34]

In the business of our salvation, it is no use keeping our eyes on our neighbor unless it is for a good example. The Spirit of God distributes His gifts as He wills. It is folly and ingratitude to quarrel with Him. Let us trade with what He has given us, and we shall lay up treasures that shall not perish.

[34] Cf. Matt. 25:22-23.

☞

Chapter Ten

Use your gifts and
possessions for God's glory

Catholics and Communists are opposed to one another on the question of property. Catholics hold that private property is lawful; Communists hold that it is unlawful, since all goods belong to the community and not to the individual. At first, the Communist might seem to have the nobler, higher, more unselfish view. But it is not so, for the Catholic holds that man is absolute owner of no property whatsoever, whether private or communal; he is only administrator. There is but one absolute Owner, who is God, the God of infinite justice and goodness.

No man, whether individually or collectively, can say, "May I not do what I like with my own?" Nothing is his own in that sense; all is God's and must be given an account of, as for property entrusted, property on loan.

The Gospel says, "The kingdom of Heaven is likened to a king who would take an account of his servants."[35] The point of this sentence lies in this: that all human property and possession is on loan, and not unconditional. In fact, the condition is very strict.

[35] Matt. 18:23.

The capital loaned by God to man must not only not be destroyed, wasted, or allowed to deteriorate, but it must be laid out to profit, and the Sovereign Master of all men will ask for the account and say, "Pay what thou owest!"[36] Should a millionaire throttle a workman, his fellow servant, for the sake of a few pennies, while he himself cannot give a proper account of his own millions, his angry Lord will insist on the last dollar in his own case.

Whatever I am and whatever I possess is only money left on trust. It is God's charity left to me and to others, and celestial Charity Commissioners will see to it that I give a most minute and detailed statement of how I spent the sum involved. The divine trust-deed allows me to use the capital — that is, my body, my mind, my will, and my earthly goods — as far as I need them for my own true progress and development to become a better man in God's sight. Whatever remains of my bodily, mental, and spiritual powers, whatever remains of my earthly goods, I am strictly bound to spend for the good of my neighbor, for God made him as well as He made me. In making me trustee over some fraction of His creation, God did not abandon His own divine ownership or a right of a searching account of my administration of His divine property.

Yet how often do we forget that we are servants, not masters? We behave as if we were not responsible to anyone for the things we are pleased to style our own. As Christians, we would, of course, not formally deny that God was our Master, but in practice, His claim is treated as an absentee lordship. Our gifts of body: health, beauty, strength; our gifts of mind: cleverness, different capacities; our gifts of earthly goods, whether bought or inherited — we regard all these things as under our absolute control, to be used as we like and with no one to say us nay.

[36] Cf. Matt. 18:28.

Use your gifts and possessions for God's glory

So many of us deliberately live in a fools' paradise. We say to ourselves that we have not actually sinned by breaking any specific commandment, and, therefore, everything must be all right. We have lived for ourselves. We have enjoyed anything that came along, but we have always paid for it. We came honestly by the money, and if a man cannot do what he likes with his money what is the world coming to?

Some seem to picture to themselves that our Lord at the Judgment will say, "You have not stolen; you have not killed; you have not committed adultery; you have not blasphemed. Come, then, you blessed of my Father and inherit the kingdom prepared for you from the beginning of the world." But they forget that the words of the Judge may run differently: "I was hungry, and you gave me not to eat, thirsty and you gave me not to drink, naked and you clothed me not. Get away from me, you cursed, into everlasting fire."[37]

Let us, then, in the use of all our gifts and possessions, remember that we are only stewards of God's property, and that unless we use them for the glory of God, for the good of our soul, and for the benefit of our neighbor, we shall have a terrible account to pay when Christ shall come to judge the living and the dead.

[37] Cf. Matt. 25:41-42.

Chapter Eleven

⌒

Let the Holy Spirit sanctify all you do

St. Paul gives us a list of seventeen ugly vices as works of the flesh: fornication, uncleanness, immodesty, luxury, idolatry, witchcrafts, enmities, contentions, emulations, wraths, quarrels, dissensions, sects, envies, murders, drunkenness, and revelings. And he lists twelve virtues as fruits of the Holy Spirit: charity, joy, peace, patience, benignity, goodness, longanimity, mildness, faith, modesty, continency, and chastity.[38] He thereby draws two portraits, the latter of the man with God's grace, the former of the man without it. Without divine grace, human nature is liable to the most ghastly deformities.

On first hearing the appalling series of loathsome vices, we would almost think that the portrait of the man without grace is overdrawn and exaggerated, but on second and deeper thought, we must recognize the truth of the description. Every individual sinner may not always commit all the crimes enumerated, but he lives in a sphere where his companions, each in his way and measure, is guilty at least of some of these things, and he is with them in their nefarious behavior. Yet the world makes a desperate

[38] Gal. 5:19-23. The RSV lists fewer vices and fruits. — ED.

attempt to show as good a face as the company of the children of God, for the purpose of showing that "religion" or "no religion" makes practically no difference in the conduct of man, that in fact man needs no divine grace to keep straight and to be a model man.

They triumphantly point to some individual who professed religion and yet showed many vices, and to another individual who lived without religion and seemed a paragon of virtue. They forget three things: first, that the comparison of one individual with one other individual does not prove any rule; second, that mere nominal profession of any religion constitutes no charter of sanctity and is no peremptory proof of the state of grace (many nominal Catholics are sinners, *in spite of* their Catholic Faith, not *because* of it); third, the constant, careful, and conscientious performance of religious duties is indeed a *prima facie* proof of the state of divine grace, and the conduct of such religious people considered as a multitude stands in glorious contrast to the multitude of those who ostentatiously neglect religion and are thus presumably not in the state of divine grace.

No Catholic holds that, without grace, a person could not perform some naturally good act, or that pagans, ancient and modern, do nothing but sin. God forbid that anyone should hold so horrible an opinion, but without grace — that is, without the Holy Spirit — nothing can be done that ultimately avails unto eternal salvation. Without grace, not even the natural law can long be kept in its integrity, nor grave temptations be successfully withstood for long.

Our unaided human nature after the Fall is so weak, our human flesh so frail, that although now and then we feel stirrings for good and may carry out an action that is naturally beautiful and right, soon we stumble into some of those loathsome seventeen things that St. Paul enumerates in his letter, and we are helplessly foundering in sin. When, therefore, people boast of the fine conduct of those who know no God or faith, let us not be deceived: not all is gold that glitters!

Or if there is genuine gold, it is the outcome of divine grace; it is a fruit of the Holy Spirit, for the outcome of mere human endeavors, even if not bad, is of lesser metal and has not sufficient value to buy life eternal.

It is the Holy Spirit who is the Sanctifier and the Giver of life. Unless He lives in our soul, a troop of demon vices will besiege our castle, and in the end, some of these demons will force entrance, triumph over our better instincts, and reduce us to the slavery of degrading sins. On the other hand, if He lives within us as His anointed temple, He will fill us with charity, joy, peace, patience, benignity, goodness, and longanimity. We shall be strong in virtue, for the strength of God will strengthen our will. The Holy One of God will sanctify our innermost being.

Do not grieve the Holy Spirit by sin and thus drive him out, for without Him, we become the prey to the fiend of mankind and the corruption of our flesh.

Chapter Twelve

⌒

Remember that only God can satisfy you

"Our sufficiency is from God":[39] these words of St. Paul show the immense strength and self-possession of the true Christian. We men have no sufficiency of ourselves, although some of us seem to think we do.

With all our shrewdness, learning, and science, we are weak things. We talk of mastering nature, but one thunderclap, one flash of lightning sends us scurrying; an epidemic mows us down by the thousands. Above all, our fellowmen are our danger; when a war comes, dynamite, bombs, and machine guns slaughter us, and no one seems to know the remedy against the stark insanity of war. And were we even sufficiently shielded against danger from without, from the forces of nature and our fellows, were we to live in absolute security, even then we would not be sufficient to ourselves. Give us food and drink, clothing and housing in abundance, give us honors, pleasures, amusements, and distractions in plenty, and we are still not satisfied. Had we all these things in profusion, we would still say to ourselves, "They are not sufficient." We would hunger still.

[39] 2 Cor. 3:5.

Try to satiate a man with every good thing the earth has to give, and he will cry out for something else, for nought can satisfy him, but God alone. Some will not acknowledge this even at the very end. They may, with scathing sarcasm, denounce the stupid pleasures of human life; they may vent their spleen in fierce words of bitter disappointment, and yet not turn to God, and thus, with a curse on their lips, depart this world.

Others happily will seek God before the end comes. They may have wandered far and gone long astray; they may have tasted and tried many things in vain, but they were taught by their sad experience and at last held out their longing hands to Heaven, where God is. Blessed are those who from childhood have learned that their sufficiency lies in God. They will be strong in adversity.

The hurricane, the epidemic, the scourge of war may not spare them, but whatever befalls them, they can bear it with fortitude, for nothing can happen but what God wills, and, in this knowledge, they find their strength. Like others, they will shed tears in pain and sorrow, but they will never be tears of despair, tears of angry helplessness, or tears of ineffective rebellion against their fate. They are not so foolish as to shake their fists against Heaven. They know too well that the sky is beyond their grasp, and that He who reigns above the cherubim cannot be terrified by their gestures. They are cast in too heroic a mold to whimper and whine against His blessed will; as true heroes, they bend their head and say, "The Lord has given, and the Lord has taken. Blessed be the name of the Lord."[40]

Moreover, their inner sufficiency lies in God. They can honestly enjoy whatever the good God sends them of the joys of this life. In fact, they enjoy them better than others do. They enjoy them in greater peace of soul, with less hectic uncertainty, and with deeper inner satisfaction, for their mind rests in God. But the

[40] Cf. Job 1:21.

enjoyment of God's temporal gifts is not their all in all. The Giver is to them more than any of His gifts. They truly love God, and love satisfies. Human lovers often disappoint; God never does. If earthly affairs are unsatisfactory and give them trouble, they always have God to fall back upon.

God has a wonderful way of comforting and sustaining those who lovingly trust in Him. The saints are excellent witnesses to this fact; a disconsolate, despairing, gloomy saint is unknown. But everyone who has tried it has experienced it in a measure, how God is "sufficient" to the human heart even on earth. In Heaven the blessed forever cry out, "Our sufficiency is from God."

Part Two

*Cultivate your
spiritual life*

Chapter Thirteen

Develop your inner life

In his letter to the Ephesians, St. Paul beseeches God that we might be strengthened by God's Spirit unto the inward man.[41] Man is apt to be satisfied when he leads an outwardly correct life, when, in word and deed, he lives according to the accepted standards of a respectable life. Man is apt to live on the surface of things without minding much the deep things of the spirit.

Blameless external behavior is the highest aim of the world. Fair is as fair does, says the world. What a man thinks is a matter of indifference.

In relation to God, matters are exactly the reverse. It is the inward man that counts. It is what a man within the depth of his mind and heart thinks and wills that is of importance. Our Lord proclaimed:

"Things which proceed out of the mouth come forth from the heart, and those things defile a man; from the heart come forth evil thoughts, murders, adulteries, thefts, false testimonies, blasphemies: these are the things that defile a man."[42]

[41] Eph. 3:16.
[42] Matt. 15:18-20.

"It was said to them of old: 'Thou shalt not kill, and whosoever shall kill shall be in danger of the judgment.' But I say to you that whosoever is angry with his brother shall be in danger of the judgment. It was said to them of old: 'Thou shalt not commit adultery.' But I say to you: whosoever shall look on a woman to lust after her hath already committed adultery with her in his heart."[43]

"Blessed are the clean of heart, for they shall see God."[44]

"The light of thy body is thy eye. If thy eye be single, thy whole body shall be full of light, but if thy eye be evil, thy whole body shall be darksome. If, then, the light that is in thee be darkness, the darkness itself, how dark shall it be!"[45]

Catholics, of course, accept our Lord's teaching in principle, but living as they do in a world where man's inner life is disregarded, and only external activity is praised or blamed, they are tempted to regard sins of thought as mere peccadilloes in comparison with sins of deed. They are tempted to belittle good intention or bad intention as long as the outward deed is correct. They will acknowledge that a man must join in public worship of God, but they will pay little heed to that inward life of prayer, which must be the very soul of all external religion.

Holy Writ mourns that the world is perishing "because there is no one who considereth in his heart";[46] no one gives himself the trouble to think. We are apt to think of sins of thought only as direct scheming and planning of a definite evil deed. This, we realize, is wrong and must be confessed, but we often forget that we may have sinned in thought by mere omission. A man must think of God, of his soul, of his eternal salvation. He must love God in his heart; it is not enough externally to praise God with

[43] Matt. 5:21-22, 27-28.
[44] Matt. 5:8.
[45] Matt. 6:22-23.
[46] Jer. 12:11.

his lips. It is wrong to fill our mind all day long with idle, useless thoughts and imaginations, to let our thoughts drift aimlessly or dangerously.

Some people dream foolish dreams of imaginary victories over imaginary foes, just to amuse their pride. Or they conjure up soft, tender scenes in imaginary company, and they live in a fabulous paradise, just to amuse their sensuous fancies. It is this voracious modern novel-reading that, spiritually speaking, gives people softening of the brain. They are not strengthened by God's spirit unto the inward man, that Christ may dwell in their hearts through faith so that they may understand the sublimity and the depth of the knowledge of the charity of Christ. They do not face the eternal truths. They dare not steadfastly look on the realities of life. They seek for soothing fiction, as if thereby they could escape the inevitable future. People seek distractions, for they are afraid to be alone and to be obliged to look into their own souls and do some vigorous thinking.

This by no means applies only to big sinners, who are terrified lest their evil past should torment them. It applies to comparatively good people without any lurid past. They float along on the stream of casual consciousness; they turn deliberately aside from any serious thought, as if it threatened trouble or might reveal some unpleasant duty. They do not think; they prefer the flimsy stuff dreams are made of. They are Christians of a kind without a truly Christian inward life. Their inward life is more pagan than Christian.

Poor creatures! They will have to start thinking sometime, for they cannot dodge death. If they save their souls by a minimum of thought on this side of the grave, they will have to do long thinking in Purgatory, where there are no newspapers, or novels, or frivolous friends, or idle gossip, or cinemas to drug men's minds as substitutes for inward life.

Chapter Fourteen

⌒

Learn to overcome
common obstacles to prayer

How is it that most of us find prayer so desperately difficult? First, because it is a thing truly difficult in itself. It is speaking to God, and it is difficult for frail and fallen man to converse with the most-high God.

Have you ever watched a child trying to keep up a conversation with a grown-up? The child will say a sentence or two; then follows an embarrassed silence for a few seconds as the child will be looking around for his toys again. So we children of God deal with our Father in Heaven. We feel an impulse to talk to Him, we actually say a few words, but ever so soon we feel awkward and out of our sphere and turn from heavenly things again to earthly ones.

We should not feel surprised or angry with ourselves. Above all, we should not in our disappointment give up on prayer altogether and say to ourselves, "It is no good. I have tried. I cannot do it. Others may find it easy; I don't." No one, except a saint, and then only sometimes, after years of patient trial, finds praying easy. But God sees our struggling and striving to speak to Him, and our very endeavor, however imperfect, is greatly pleasing to Him.

A blessing on those who continue to try, for the persistent trial is loving homage to God. It is like the somewhat incoherent prattle of a child, the little jerks and stammers of an infant that are music to the ear of a father.

A blight falls on those who cease to try. They prayed perhaps when they were young, but when they came to man's or woman's estate, they discontinued the practice of their youth and began a dreary, barren, prayerless life, and their soul withered and died. In cowardly slovenliness, they dropped prayer because it required effort. They lost God, because they couldn't be bothered.

Another reason we find prayer so difficult lies, not in prayer itself, but in ourselves. We misunderstand. We imagine prayer to be an elaborate ceremonial affair, a matter of sonorous and stately words, a thing that can hardly be done without a prayer book, a thing that seems to require Sunday clothes! We behave as if God were some Eastern potentate, who must not be approached without knowledge of court etiquette, as if praying in a bus, tram, or subway were an irreverence.

We say we have no time to go into a church to pray — perhaps sometimes we speak the truth in saying so — and it does not dawn upon us that we might pray in the kitchen, or we might be praying while washing ourselves in the morning. We need not first look respectable before we place ourselves in the presence of God. God is not particularly impressed by smart clothes. God willingly hears a man who prays in his shirtsleeves or a woman who prays in an apron that has seen better days.

It may be difficult to stay for an hour in still meditation, but it is not so difficult to raise our mind for a minute or two scores of times during the day. Our prayer may be almost wordless, no definite sentences need be formed, but our heart would be lifted up toward God were we only to think: "Lift up your heart." Suppose a man or a woman deliberately said — not uttering a word, but only thinking in his or her heart — "God help me to believe in You, hope in

You, and love You!" Such a man or woman, if persevering in this practice, would be on the high road to sanctity, for sanctity is obtained and maintained by prayer.

But there is a third thing that makes prayer difficult: it is our conscious clinging to some sin or fault that we have recognized as such. A man says, "I do not know what has come over me. I seem to be unable to pray!" Friend, examine your conscience. Are you hugging some sinful affection or some sinful aversion and will not give it up? More especially: have you a feeling of hatred toward some brother, a feeling of contempt and disdain for some neighbor? Have you done them some harm and will not repair it? Has your brother offended you and you will not forgive him?

No wonder you cannot pray, my friend. It is God's warning to you that something is amiss. Before prayer, prepare your heart, says the Scripture.[47] A heart with guile, envy, or hatred, a heart with some sin lurking within, a sin that we do not want to see, but we know quite well is somehow there: such a heart is ill prepared for prayer.

But how so? Must I not pray because I am a sinner? Yes, indeed, you must pray for repentance, for the grace to overcome sin, but not with the pretense that you see not the evil, which God sees within.

Is all dryness in prayer, therefore, a sign that I am in sin and out of God's grace? No, a thousand times no! If, after honest self-examination, we find no sin deliberately cherished, we turn to God with strong, happy confidence even though prayer is a matter of effort and labor, determined to serve Him in sunshine and in darkness, in fair weather and in foul, knowing that he who perseveres unto the end shall receive the crown of life.[48]

---

[47] Eccles. 18:23 (RSV = Sir. 18:23).

[48] James 1:12.

☞

Chapter Fifteen

Pray even for small things

A class of Catholic schoolchildren was expecting its annual outing the next day. The weather had long been uncertain, and the
class was storming Heaven with prayers for sunshine. A scoffer in
the street, passing the open windows of the classroom, heard the
drone of their voices. With a superior, disdainful smile, he mur-
mured, "That won't help much. The barometer is falling."

Was the man right? Is such prayer useless and pardonable only
in children, since God is bound to respect the barometer? The
man would probably plead that if the law of atmospherics were interfered with, the whole machinery of the universe would come
asunder. To this, even a child could answer that his mother raises
the temperature considerably in the house when it gets cold in the
winter, and therefore God could probably make a little sunshine
without smashing the universe. But if God interfered just to please
the children, it would be a miracle! Yes, quite so, it would.

Is it so unlikely that God would perform a miracle for what we
regard as a trifle? Remember how God changed water into wine in
Cana in Galilee to supply some extra wine at a wedding party.[49] A

---

[49] John 2:1-11.

children's outing may appear to God as important as a little jollity at a marriage feast. What, in fact, is really big in God's eyes, and what is small? All things are equally easy to infinite power. None of our important affairs are really formidable to God. God cannot be daunted by the magnitude of our request, nor can He be offended by their littleness, as if they are beneath His notice.

Let us bear this truth in mind. It is a queer superstition to think that God must not be bothered by trifles, as if He were too busy to be able to attend to every detail. It is a worse error still to imagine that God's goodness and patience run out when we dare to ask too much. Christ Himself taught us importunity in begging when He spoke this parable: "Who of you, having a friend, shall go to him at midnight and say, 'Friend, lend me three loaves, for a friend of mine on a journey has come to me, and I have not what to set before him.' But he from within should answer, 'Trouble me not. The door is now shut, and my children are with me in bed. I cannot rise and give thee.' Yet if he shall continue knocking, I say to you, although he will not rise and give him because he is his friend, yet because of his importunity, he will rise and give him as many as he needeth."[50]

This homely parable urges us to affectionate persistence in prayer, as it were compelling the Divine Goodness to grant our request. But is there not something unseemly and reprehensible in urging a request for a temporal favor? No, certainly not, unless we fall into one of two faults.

Some petitioners almost threaten God with their displeasure if He will not grant the particular thing they want. They are like petulant, unpleasant children who start sulking because they do not get the toy they fancy. "If I do not get this, I shall never pray for anything again," say some people in silly, bad humor. When their request seems definitely refused, they lessen their pieties, prayers,

[50] Luke 11:5-8.

and devotions as an unspoken sort of revenge for not being heard. In a kind of angry despair, they say to God that if He is deaf to their entreaties, they won't talk to Him anymore. They are like babies in a tantrum. That is not the way to wheedle Infinite Love.

Tell the Father almighty that you want a thing very, very much, and that He is sure to give it to you if it is good for you, and that if you do not get it, you will still lovingly kiss His hands, for He knows best.

Another fault is to be so absorbed in the wish for some temporal thing as to forget to ask for spiritual things first. We are apt to plague Almighty God perpetually with prayers for good health and good luck in our business, for success in this undertaking or that, in escaping this punishment, this danger, this accident or that, but rare are our prayers for the welfare of our soul, for an increase of sanctifying grace, for strength in temptation, for laying up treasures in Heaven, which thieves cannot steal or moth and rust destroy.[51] We ask for bodily health while our soul is sick; we ask for money while our soul is poor in grace. We are not unlike delirious patients, who clamor for sweets instead of for medicine.

Indeed, let us ask God for temporal gifts, but all things in proportion and measure. Let us mind the things of the kingdom of Heaven first, and all other things shall be added unto us.[52]

[51] Matt. 6:19.
[52] Cf. Matt. 6:33.

Chapter Sixteen

⌒

Seek continual spiritual renewal

Christ's Resurrection from the dead was the beginning of God's brave new world, the joyous triumph over the death, and the decay of the old world of fallen man and over the age-long bondage under sin and the old serpent, the Devil. The Church repeats her Easter festivities — blessing new light, new fire, new waters for the font, and new sacred oils for the sacraments — every year and thereby signifies that the life of man's soul needs perpetual renovation, an incessant overcoming and a casting off of the old, a replacing of worn-out habits by new ones and reaching forward to greater things in the future than in the past.

It is an unfortunate illusion among many that the spiritual life is just a "going on as you are." If you are in the state of grace, just continue doing what you are accustomed to and avoid sin — that is all there is to it, they say. But they are wrong. Neither human nature nor grace acts in that way. Human nature is not just a clock wound up, going without variation its allotted time. Grace is not doled out by God in precise, invariable quantities at precisely spaced moments. Life needs infusion of fresh energies. The soul must sometimes have an Easter day. It must shake itself free from what clogs its progress, all that deadly encumbrance of routine, that cloying, all-enveloping sluggishness which comes to all of us, unless, by a vigorous determined effort, aided by grace, we rouse ourselves to make a fresh start.

We need the brisk, sacred novelty of Easter. We read in the Scriptures that Christ says unto the blessed in Heaven, "Behold, I make all things new."[53] May the risen Christ come to us on earth and say, "Behold, I make all things new!" *Come to us, glorious Master, and raise us up to newness of life!*

We were buried, if not in grosser sins, yet under a multitude of lesser sins and failings, and unless grace stirs us up, the stone of our self-chosen grave will never be rolled away.

We are buried in selfishness; we must be taken out of ourselves. We are buried in worldliness; we must be lifted above this world. We are buried in sensuousness, love of ease and comfort, if not worse things; we must be rescued and set gloriously free. We are buried in somnolent sloth in regard to spiritual things: we may still go through the routine of our prayers and sacraments, but they have become as lifeless things to us; we must be quickened and filled with energy. We are buried under a load of mean, ugly — so-called venial — sins, sins of envy, anger, untruthfulness, covetousness, and whatever the names of our many failings may be; we must, by God's grace, work our way out into the fresh air of Easter morn.

We may have been buried in the slough of despondency — even good people sometimes are; it is moodiness of temperament. We must overcome our sadness and shout for joy our *alleluia*, for Christ is risen indeed.

In His Resurrection is our strength; in His Resurrection is our hope. He is the Hero who conquered sin and death, not only for Himself, but for us. The vigor of Christ's risen life is ours through our union with Him. In a sense, the whole of mankind on Easter

---

[53] Apoc. 21:5 (RSV = Rev. 21:5).

morn rose from the dead, for then was the power of sin broken and the Devil, the slave-master of humanity, routed. But we should appropriate the grace of Easter to ourselves, for God, who created us independently of ourselves, will not save us without ourselves.

For many people, Christ suffered, died, and rose in vain, because they refuse to turn to Him, the source of all spiritual power, the wellspring of all endeavors that makes for virtue and holiness. They will not share His victory, but idly trust in their own efforts, as if sin could be conquered without Him, as if they could smite Satan without Him who smote him from the Cross and undid all his might when the sun rose on Resurrection day.

In the risen Christ is all our hope. It is as St. Paul said to the Corinthians: "If Christ be not risen again, then our preaching is vain, and your faith is vain, and you are still in your sins."[54]

In happy pride we can conclude our Creed with the words "I believe in the resurrection of the body and in life everlasting."

Had Christ not risen, we would still have no more than the dim, uncertain hope of the Patriarchs of the Old Testament, and our departure would be like unto a journey into a land of shadows. The sun that shone on the open tomb is the sun that shines on the children of the New Covenant.

---

[54] 1 Cor. 15:13-14.

◌

Chapter Seventeen

Let the Holy Spirit assist and console you

A catechism class was asked what a paraclete was. After some embarrassed silence, a boy piped up: "A bird, Father!" Whether the little man confused *paraclete* with *parakeet*, or thought of the Dove at our Lord's Baptism, posterity will never know, but it is not unlikely that if the question were asked of adults, answers as erroneous and as quaint would be forthcoming. In St. John's Gospel, our Lord uses the word *Paraclete* four times, but in the Douay version, that Greek word remains untranslated, because it is so rich in meaning that it is difficult to find a single modern word to render it.

Fundamentally it means someone called to one's aid in need or distress — hence, a helper, an assistant, one who intervenes to comfort, support, and console, a person summoned in a great emergency. Now, popular use in our Lord's day had it that the word was applied to the lawyer, the barrister, who spoke for you, pleaded for you in a court case — your legal representative, in fact. Outside legal practice, it came to mean an intercessor, a beneficent go-between, a mediator. In Latin we have almost the exact equivalent: an advocate.

In the tender discourse the evening before His death, our Lord repeatedly referred to the Paraclete who was about to come. We are bound to think that our Lord, by that mysterious name for the Holy Spirit, meant to convey all the richness of meaning that the word contains. Christ is our "Advocate with the Father,"[55] as the Scripture saith, and the Holy Spirit is "another advocate"[56] or paraclete. Christ is our advocate because, as man, He pleads for us men, ever interceding for us at the throne of His Father. The Holy Spirit did not become man; hence, He speaks for us in another way. He speaks for us because He is what He is: the subsistent personal love of the infinite God.

God is holiness, God is power, God is justice, and these dread attributes are, as it were, arranged against us, who are stained, weak, sinful, fallen creatures. It is the Love of God that must speak for us, or we are lost. "If Thou, O Lord, regard iniquities, Lord, who shall abide it?"[57] So we plead, or rather it is the Holy Spirit, dwelling in us through grace, who pleads within us. "The Spirit helpeth our infirmity," writes St. Paul, "for we know not what we should pray for as we ought, but the Spirit Himself asketh for us with unspeakable groanings, and He that searcheth the hearts knoweth what the Spirit desireth."[58]

Thus, the third Person of the Blessed Trinity, who, through Baptism and Confirmation, has made our soul a temple of God in which He has His permanent abode through grace, speaks and pleads within us, since all our prayers are prompted by Him, directed by Him, and worthy of acceptance through Him. Thus, He acts as our Advocate, whose eloquence moves the heart of God. Without His grace, all would be idle pleading, unworthy of an answer, for man left to himself without the indwelling of the Holy Spirit has no voice that can reach the throne of God.

[55] 1 John 2:1.
[56] John 14:16.
[57] Cf. Ps. 129:3 (RSV = Ps. 130:3).
[58] Rom. 8:26-27.

Let the Holy Spirit assist and console you

O Paraclete,
put Thy words upon my lips,
and mingle Thy voice with mine.
Teach me to speak the language of God,
so that, through Thy pleading by me and in me,
I may obtain the mercy of the eternal Father above!
Be to me not only an Advocate,
but a Comforter, Thou of all Consolers best!

More people are lost by despondency than by pride, unless perchance despair is itself a kind of hidden pride. Thousands made feeble attempts at goodness, but then throw it all up in despair. The road to Heaven is long and hard, and the occasions of stumbling, the actual falls, falls perhaps deep and degrading, have been so many that the lonesome traveler on the path of life can hope for no happy end of his journey unless some companion will appear to comfort him and raise in him confidence and sureness of Heaven.

Such a companion may be a fellowman, but the comfort he can give is but little. He may whisper sympathy and good advice, but he cannot give inner strength; he cannot give the power of grace. We need a divine Comforter for our souls, one who can enter the very depth of our being and, while knowing us through and through, love us and bear us up.

It is the Paraclete of Pentecost we want, who, with flames of fire, will set our soul alight and change us from sorrowful failures into bright and blissful children of God. Every one of us sometimes suffers from dark depression, when we crave for the word of a friend to cheer us and infuse into us the courage we lack, which we feel we so sorely need. Then is our time to sink on our knees and say, "Come, Holy Spirit":

Friend of my soul, come
and encompass with Thy power
my mind and heart.

Heal, strengthen, and raise me
with that spiritual comfort
which Thou alone canst give,
that I may run again in
the joy of Thy divine grace
along the road of life and
reach at last the land of the living,
where, in happiness untold,
all adore Thee, Lord and Life-giver,
who, with the Father and the Son,
rulest and reignest for ever. Amen.

Part Three

Live your Faith

Chapter Eighteen

⁀

Find peace and joy in your Faith

St. Paul wishes us all "peace and joy in believing."[59] Undoubtedly Christians believe terrifying and fearsome truths, truths apt to take away a man's peace and joy. The dread justice of the all-holy God, the awfulness of sin, and the appalling alternative between eternal happiness and eternal sorrow make a man tremble when he thinks of them. Christians are often scoffed at by unbelievers, as if they perpetually lived in a nightmare of eternal damnation and were ever shivering before a pitiless judge.

As a matter of fact, the reverse is the case. The Christian finds peace and joy in believing. The truths just mentioned he does indeed accept. They are truths that even his natural reason suggests, and they face the non-Christian as much as the Christian, however much the infidel may be trying not to think of them, or to conjure up for himself a fools' paradise from which death will suddenly expel him.

But the Christian, in addition to these natural truths, believes, through God's revelation, three truths that fill him with peace and with joy and change what might become a nightmare into a

---

[59] Rom. 15:13.

happy waking and waiting for the dawn. These three truths are the love of God, the forgiveness of sin, and the promise of everlasting joy.

First, the Christian believes in the love of God. God so loved the world that He gave His only-begotten Son unto death, yea, unto the death of the Cross.[60] Reason reveals God as Creator and Judge; faith reveals Him as a tender Father who encompasses mankind with infinite love. Who, by unaided reason, could ever have guessed that God cared so much for wayward feeble man that He would come from Heaven, assume our nature, live among us, and go through the agony of Gethsemane and the torment and death of Calvary to redeem us from eternal loss? An immense peace and joy enters the human heart of him who believes that Infinite Love broods over all the multitude of the children of men.

The crucifix, in itself so ghastly and gruesome a sight, has become the loveliest portrayal of God's unspeakable love. In every home, in every room where that image hangs, the outstretched arms of God incarnate seem to embrace all those who place their trust in Him who was crucified for them. A sense of security and calm descends on all who are of strong faith, for they know that the omnipotence of God is like the power of a friend and a brother to them. No one hath greater love than he who gives his life for a friend, we say; but God has gone further: He has given His life for us when we were as yet His enemies.

The Christian believes in the forgiveness of sins. A man's sins are a burden to him, and only a few rogues or fools pretend that it is not so. The memory of one's many faults and sins is a terrifying torment to many. Even those who are not precisely criminals, but might be counted among so-called decent and respectable people, feel that there has been and is much in their lives that disturbs

[60] John 3:16; Phil. 2:8.

them, that robs their mind of rest and their heart of full peace and joy.

Who shall undo our sins? Does God ever pardon, or must I carry my guilt about with me always and only wait for the bitter punishment? It is an insoluble problem for the mere natural man; hence, he is haunted by that tormenting doubt as to whether there is pity and pardon on high.

The Christian knows indeed that he is a sinner, but he also knows that God forgives. The man on the Cross at the right hand of Christ tells him so; the woman cowering at the foot of the Cross tells him so. The man was a murderer and a highway robber who knew that his death was richly deserved; the woman was once a public sinner in her town. But both were forgiven; their sin was undone.

The thought of the penitent thief and of Mary Magdalene lifts a burden from a sinner's soul. God forgives those who repent. A ray of light enters a once-darkened soul; peace and joy, so long banished, re-enter, and a blessed calm begins to reign where formerly there was turmoil and the bitterness of ugly memories. The joy of forgiven sin is an all-pervading exquisite joy, exceeding any earthly pleasure.

Lastly, the Christian believes in the divine promise of everlasting joy. The youngest child learns of everlasting joy. The youngest child learns it in the catechism: "*Why did God make you?* God made me to know Him, love Him, and serve Him in this world and to be happy with Him forever in the next."

For a Christian, the horizon is always red as a pledge of the glorious sun of the coming day. There may be darknesses and storm clouds, cold and sleet, or heat and oppressiveness during his life's day, but for the Christian, all's well that ends well, if, through God's grace, the intercession of God's Mother, and all the saints, he has been made worthy of the promises of Christ. Christ will not fail him. His sure hope lies in Him. No one can steal his inheritance from him. He is heir of God and joint-heir with Christ.[61] He is full of peace and joy in believing. "Your joy shall be full, and your joy no one shall take from you," said his Master.[62] The Christian believes it, and he is a happy man.

[61] Rom. 8:17.
[62] Cf. John 16:22; 17:13.

Chapter Nineteen

⁓

Conform your actions to your Faith

When Israel passed out of Egypt, a miraculous cloud, visible by day and lightsome by night, acted as their guide. By an astounding wonder, the sea was opened, and they passed through dry-shod, while it closed on their foes, Pharaoh and his army.

In the desert, they received food from Heaven and drink from the rock that Moses struck. Thus God showered His blessings upon them in marvelous abundance — "yet with most of them God was not well pleased." This is a fearsome warning even for us Christians, the chosen people of God's new and eternal covenant.

We are indeed the elect, favorites of God, and have received greater blessings than Israel of old. Christ, the Light of the World, goes before us in the illumination of the true Faith. We have escaped out of the bondage of Egypt, the bondage of sin and the Devil, through the waters of Baptism. We have received a greater Manna from Heaven than was given to the Jews in the desert.

The Jews of old boasted that no nation had its god closer and nearer to itself than God was to Israel. We have a greater boast still in our Emmanuel, our God-with-us, in the Blessed Sacrament of the altar. Israel's covenant with God through the sacrificial blood that Moses sprinkled was but a frail thing, a pale and passing thing compared with our covenant with God through the Blood of Christ. The Blood of Christ once shed on the Cross is offered on the altar daily as the years and the centuries roll on. And yet have we not a dread that perhaps it might be said, "With most of us God is not well pleased"?

The story of Christendom in the past and the present — I mean that vast multitude that calls itself Christian and is baptized — is sad and disconcerting reading. No doubt there have been and are tens of thousands of saints. There are myriads of humble, hidden, simple families on which God's eyes rest with pleasure, for they love Him truly and serve Him. On the other hand, well-nigh innumerable is the motley crowd of nominal Christians, and bold would be the man who dared to proclaim with certainty, "With most of us God is very well pleased."

Christendom is a strange sight! Marvels of sanctity are certainly not wanting; examples of faithfulness, purity, charity, and heroism are undoubtedly visible; but distressingly great is the number of those who disgrace the Christian name. Many there are who say, "Lord, Lord," but do not the will of the Father who is in Heaven,[63] who do daily the things that are grievously displeasing in the sight of God. So numerous are they that we almost fear the verdict on Christendom: with most of them God is not well pleased.

How easily we are satisfied with just the external profession of our Faith, with the performance of outward duties of religion, but how careless as to whether our conduct corresponds with our high profession.

We may be called practicing Catholics in regard to the observance of our church duties, but even then we may belong to the large class with whom God is not well pleased. God wants a Christian life. God wants chastity, kindness, and truth. We are not dispensed from those just because we have been to Sunday Mass.

[63] Matt. 7:21.

God hates envy, selfishness, anger, lying, impurity, and dishonesty. We are not pleasing to Him unless we fulfill all the commandments. The first commandment is indeed the first, but there are nine others. The observance of the first does not release us from the others, any more than the observance of the other nine is sufficient without the first, as the irreligious modern man seems to think.

Let us enter into ourselves and scrutinize our conscience to see whether, notwithstanding our name of Catholic and our membership in the Church of God, God may not reckon us with the great crowd on whom His displeasure rests. We Catholics are in perpetual danger of conforming in behavior and outlook on life to the pagan world that surrounds us, without, however, leaving the Catholic Church as Christian denomination. Human nature can be so strangely inconsistent that some may be fierce, militant Catholics, ready to raise their fist against anyone who would dare to breathe a word against the Pope or the priests and yet merit God's wrath by their uncatholic lives. Cheating in business, using mean tricks in trade, these men of foul lips and coarse speech are loose in their morals, are cruel to relatives, make their home a hell, are slothful and unreliable, live on the earnings of others, are boastful, intolerant, vengeful, and in fact, perpetually provoke God's displeasure and are a disgrace to God's kingdom on earth to which they nominally give adhesion.

Not, indeed, that it would be better for them to leave the Church — God forbid — but it would be good if they recalled that unless they repent, their marvelous privileges on earth, however great, are in themselves no title of admission to the Promised Land of Heaven. To be delivered out of Egypt and even to eat the heavenly Manna is not identical with entrance into the Palestine of God. May God give us perseverance unto the end.

~

Chapter Twenty

Form your political views
according to your Faith

"Catholics should keep out of politics!" The answer to this slogan is simple: it cannot be done. With all the world around us talking and thinking politics, even our very silence becomes politics, whether of approval or disapproval or indifference, and even the assertion of indifference is politics. What, then, should a Catholic do?

The Catholic Church has no divine commission to guide people in the choice of plans for the temporal welfare of people, as long as these plans are equally in conformity with the divine moral law. Thereby, however, Catholics are not released from all responsibility for their political opinions and activities. Let us take a parallel case.

The Catholic Church does not teach medicine or hygiene, but this does not mean that the Catholic has no duties and responsibilities toward his own body. A Catholic is responsible to God for all he thinks, says, and does. There is no exemption for politics, whether home or international politics. Politics are not a matter of whim or fancy, like choosing your sweets. They should not be ruled by passion or sloth, or mere family pride or tradition, or mere personal interest and selfishness, or so-called class-consciousness. They should be ruled by the wish to do God's will and to promote the good of our fellowmen and not exclusively those of our own nation or of our own class.

What rules, then, should a Catholic follow in his public life, since every Catholic, however simple and seemingly unimportant, has some public life?

First and foremost: He must remember that temporal values are subordinate to spiritual and eternal ones. Not infrequently he stands before the choice between some immediate temporal benefit to some section of the community and the certain spiritual harm of many. Many unscrupulous politicians dangle some such bait before the eyes of the public in order to gain adherents, while it is obvious that their gain of power will be a disaster to the moral and religious state of their nation. The reason some nations have vile governments is that Catholics are so often caught in this snare. They greedily swallow the bait and say, "Ah well, religion will somehow look after itself!" Or worse still, "One should not mix religion with politics," as if for a Catholic there could be anything he should not mix religion with! We Catholics stand toward all patriotisms and politics in a different way from that of other people. For us, these things are not ultimate values. They are values, yes, but not supreme values. In the last resort, it is God and the souls of men that matter, and nothing else. "What doth it profit a man if he gain the whole world and suffer the loss of his own soul?"[64]

The second rule is: Let us not do evil that good may come. "All is permitted in love and war," runs the proverb; some people would add "and politics." Untruths are told, or wretched half-truths and portentous exaggerations to damage the reputation or the cause of opponents. We pick up our newspaper, the paper that is supposed

[64] Matt. 16:26.

to uphold our views, and we greedily accept all it tells us to the detriment of the other party or the other nation. A lie is, after all, a lie, even if it is propaganda. The readers half-suspect that the thing is not true, but they retail it with embellishments to the next man they meet, until the opponent becomes a monster of iniquity, even though, as a matter of fact, he is just an ordinary man, who honestly thinks differently from us.

Or the contrary takes place: Our own party is guilty of vile practices, but because we agree with their aims, we hide the truth by silence or invent lame excuses or even lie to shield them.

The third and last rule: Let our politics be a matter of conscience for us and be supported by prayer. Let us not take sides until we are sure we are well informed. True, we cannot all be experts, but we can all in our own measure obtain reliable information rather than be led by passionate speeches by men of doubtful antecedents. It is not the heart only that should move us, but the head also. Sudden bursts of anger, or even of indignation and pity, cannot always be trusted to be the voice of wisdom.

If sometimes we cannot settle our doubts, let us ask advice, and when all other things are equal, the advice of a good practicing Catholic, of a priest, or of a Catholic paper is more likely to lead to the truth than other counselors are.

⌒

Chapter Twenty-One

Beware of false prophets

"Beware of false prophets" the Gospel warns.[65] When we hear of false prophets, we are apt to imagine some cunning and leering individual in outlandish garb propounding in public some sinful but seductive theory and making lying promises about the future. Perchance we are picturing to ourselves some atheistic ranter, with disheveled hair, contorted features, and snarling mouth, shrieking or bawling out disgusting blasphemies.

We do not so often realize that that neat and harmless-looking fellow we see so much of at work, that spruce and well-spoken clerk who is with us at the office, or, maybe, that very efficient, apparently sensible, attractive woman who is often at our home, that charming, silver-tongued person next door who often comes in and sets forth her bright ideas about things in general — we do not realize, I say, that any of these might possibly be false prophets. We say to ourselves that their talk is only common sense, and sometimes very amusing. Their ideas are certainly advanced, a bit bold and risky perhaps, but on the whole not unsound. After all, we must keep abreast of the times, so we argue with ourselves.

---

[65] Matt. 7:15.

We hardly notice how profoundly we are influenced by their talk. We have an uneasy feeling sometimes that our outlook on things has changed somewhat since we listened to these people, and we have a slight suspicion that our opinions are not precisely those of holy Church; we feel pretty certain that our priests would not share them. We peevishly remark that we cannot be expected always to hold on to other people's apron strings and that we have a right to think for ourselves.

To think for ourselves! That is precisely what we have *not* done.

We have not thought for ourselves. Someone else has put ideas into our head, and we flatter ourselves by thinking they are our own. A false prophet has visited us, and we have fallen for him or for her. By slow doses, alien ideas have been instilled in our mind, and we have taken the dope. Now, under the influence of the drug, we are proudly prating, as parrots echoing other people's words. Satan has gulled us by his innocent-looking mask. Of course there have always been false prophets in the world, but rarely more than now. Satan will not disdain any factory-hand or scullery-maid as his prophet if they can serve his purpose.

Since false prophets may be lurking anywhere, how shall we beware of them?

First, let us remember that truth is eternal. When any man or woman comes to us with the customary claptrap that the old truths are out of date, we had better look for the mark of the beast on his forehead.[66] Truth does not change, and whosoever suggests that it does comes from the Devil. Listen to a man who says, "What I say to you is true," but laugh at the man who says, "What I say to you is new." Novelty is no proof of truth; rather the reverse, for truth is very old. The fundamental principles of human conduct do not change, for human nature does not change in spite of

[66] Cf. Apoc. 13:16 (RSV = Rev. 13:16).

all the learned nonsense of evolution. God's revelation does not change, for God does not change His mind.

Christianity is the final, immutable revelation of God to man, and if the Catholic Church after twenty centuries has not found out what it means, no self-styled modern prophet is likely to have discovered it. Therefore, when a man or a woman comes along with an unheard-of interpretation, it stands self-condemned. The person is only a juggler with words; he is not a real prophet, and if he is inspired, you can be certain that it is not by the Holy Spirit.

The second test for a false prophet is to ask yourself these questions: Does his message make me restless, discontented, or envious? Does it stir my anger, my covetousness, or my sensuousness? Under cover of fair words, does it really play upon my frailty, and when the excitement of the novelty has worn off, does it leave me unhappy and dissatisfied with myself?

If so, there is something wrong with it. God's truth brings peace and strength of soul. It may be at first hard to hear, and it may make serious and stern demands on us, but if listened to and acted upon, it leaves a blessing behind in a restfulness, a steadiness, and a deep quiet that penetrates and holds our innermost heart.

"By their fruits you shall know them," says the Gospel.[67] When the Devil speaks, he creates a feverish, sickly, evil excitement in the minds of his listeners. When God speaks, a freshness as from the eternal mountains enters our soul. Examine yourself: since you have been listening to this prophet and following his suggestions, are you a better man or a better woman for it, purer, holier, more patient, more charitable, more Christlike, or not? You may know some followers of this prophet: are they better than their fellowmen? If not, his prophecy is worthless or worse.

[67] Matt. 7:16.

Third, the Catholic should forthwith ask himself, "Who says this? Who propounds this scheme? Is he known to be, in his own person, a good man, a moral man, an honest man?"

Often we hear this: "I do not care who says it. It is jolly clever; it is very smart; it is acute enough, whoever says it. A man's private life has nothing to do with the theory he proposes. He may be right."

We reply: He may, quite, but also he may not. If he is a bad-living man, if his associates form a very doubtful company, the first reaction of a good Christian is to be on his guard, for although such people's ideas need not always be wrong, they very often are; they have presumption against them. We need not start a detective agency in the private life of authors, but not infrequently their lives are a matter of notoriety.

Furthermore, their whole outlook on life is often known. Say they are not Catholics, or worse still, apostate Catholics — perhaps they are known as unbelievers and agnostics; they deny or doubt the existence of God, and the personal survival of the human soul; their views on morality are known to be exceedingly broad; and so on. In such a case, a prudent Catholic does not retort, "All that has nothing to do with this particular theory of theirs, which seems fine and shrewd." The prudent Catholic says, "The speech is plausible, but it is certainly not recommended by the character of the speaker. It is possible, of course, that he is right, but I shall have to look very closely into it before I give my name to it or in any way accept it."

In the great majority of cases, however, we know nothing whatever of the speaker or writer. The theory was explained to us in a chance conversation, or we read it in an unsigned article in a newspaper, or even if we read the name of the author, his name conveys nothing to us. Then the prudent Catholic thinks, "The thing seems fair, but I would like to know a little more of the people who put it forward before I adopt it and make it my own."

It is ludicrous, were it not so distressing, to meet a man who has just heard or read something and is all agog with excitement. He says that his Faith has received a shock; he says he cannot understand how the Catholic Church can say or do this or that, how Christianity can be reconciled with science on this point or that. You ask him who said or wrote this, and he, with babyish naïveté, answers, "Oh, some fellow or other. I forget his name, but he seemed up in these things. I am not an expert in these matters."

O pitiful innocence! As if the world were not full of charlatans, who pose as Christ and the prophets, who want to "improve on" Christianity and want it restated in the terms of modern man!

A few years ago, a Catholic father wished me to come and see his son, aged nineteen, who declared all religion a "washout." On meeting this youthful philosopher, I was brushed aside with a lordly gesture and a haughty mien. "No good," said he, "I have read! I have read!" When I meekly remarked that I had also read and had had over forty more years to do it than he, he only gave me a pitying glance, rose, and left, repeating, "I have read."

Poor lad! He had seen something in print and taken it forthwith for absolute truth, and was eagerly following some silly, self-styled prophet to a sham "brave new world." Let us pray and watch in this deceitful world, lest we be led astray from the true Christ, who alone is the way, the truth, and the life.

⌒

Chapter Twenty-Two

Do not be deceived by flattery

Pharisees and Herodians consulted together on how to ensnare Christ in His speech. They had come to the conclusion that excessive flattery would be the best means. They came and smirked and smiled and said, "Master, we know that Thou art a true speaker, neither carest Thou for any man, for Thou dost not regard the person of men."[68] In other words: "You are outspoken; You are brave and independent; You are afraid of no one; You are a true master, and we know it." Careful and insidious flattery to elicit some imprudent words!

Our Lord saw through their cunning device and eluded their snares, but no one can deny that clever flattery is a well-known trick of hypocrisy, a trick that has succeeded with many to their utter undoing.

Not that all flattery is always wrong and to be avoided. There is a flattery that is not only permissible, but a gentle act of kindness. It is a pointing out of a person's gifts and virtues that still remains within the boundary of truth. It is a glossing over of a person's disadvantages and failings, which it would be cruel and foolish to

---

[68] Matt. 22:16.

emphasize. There is a flattery that is perfectly sincere, prompted by genuine good feeling. It draws a rosy picture of all that can be said in favor of a person in order to help him or her, to give courage or overcome depression. It is the expression of love and of admiration for what can genuinely be loved and admired, even if there are other things and other aspects that are ugly and blameworthy, which it would be unwise and perhaps even unjust to mention.

Some people boast that they cannot flatter. It is a sorry boast. It usually means that their normal inclination is to carp and criticize. They are censorious and proud. They think they demean themselves if they stress the good qualities of their neighbor.

Be all this as it may, flattery is often a mean trick and low deception to make a person grant or do what he could not be made to do by straightforward means. It is a disgraceful trading on a man's weakness and is often accompanied by mockery of the man behind his back. It is often a series of stupid untruths or exaggerations for an ignoble purpose; a profession of admiration for selfish ends.

Who does not know Aesop's fable of the fox and the crow? The crow had a big dainty morsel in his beak, but he was high up in the tree, and the hungry fox was at the foot. The fox professed passionate admiration for the crow's voice and assured him in fact that he was languishing to hear it once more. The crow was flattered and opened his beak to sing his best song, and the dainty morsel fell into the maw of the fox below. Not a bad parable of what happens among men again and again.

The shrewd simplicity of some men makes them ask, when the flattery is laid on thick, whether the flatterer wants to borrow something, but in many more cases, flattery succeeds and makes people do foolish things of which they are later ashamed. If the thing done is only just childishly foolish, it may be that no great harm is done, but not rarely the deed is disgraceful and downright sinful.

Men are told that they are broadminded, that they are of strong character, that they hold on to the apron strings of no one, that independent spirits expect much from them. Church and priest, dogma and discipline are good for the common herd, but men of such intellect and insight as they, are, to a large extent, their own law and master, and so on, and so on — until the poor fellows really believe it and preen themselves on their superiority.

There are Pharisees and Herodians enough today to ensnare a gullible person by subtle flattery. May God make us suspicious of flattery from the mouths of worldlings and make us see ourselves as we are in His sight, for the praise of God alone will shine on us when the clouds of human deception have gone.

⌒

Chapter Twenty-Three

Do not seek worldly honor

We learn in the Gospel that our Lord, after the most amazing miracle of the feeding of the five thousand, knowing that they would come and make Him king, fled to the mountain by Himself alone.[69] When a crown was held out to Him, He fled and hid, for He preferred the Cross; instead of honor, He preferred the shame. A rebuking example to all praise- and publicity-seekers.

Let anyone read history and dare to deny that the thirst for glory has been one of the chief sources of human misery and that nearly all the battlefields of the world testify that someone wanted to make himself king, wanted to lord it over his fellowmen, and gathered around him the deluded victims of his ambition. The earth has been drenched with streams of human blood to satisfy "honor," not true honor, but only some paltry piece of vanity and ostentation, some style or title that was sheer bombast. No doubt all of us would readily grant this and join in the condemnation of the insensate folly of so many of the world's grandees.

But not so many of us realize that, in our limited sphere, we may be as silly and as culpable honor-seekers as they. The endeavor

---

[69] John 6:15.

to outshine our neighbor, to be the talk of our surroundings, to receive bows and obsequious smiles in the marketplace, to sniff up a little incense of extravagant praise: that is a foible not unknown to very many of us.

This is the age of "championships," of intense rivalries between those who hold the "title," be it only of table-tennis or hockey. The craving for publicity has become a veritable craze. It has been said that people have committed suicide for the sake of notoriety and were consoled for the trouble of dying by the thought that their name and portrait would be in the papers the next morning. Vanity is an ancient and deep-rooted malady of mankind.

Two thousand years ago, our Lord spoke against those who loved to be saluted in public and be called "Rabbi," those who gave their alms at the corners of streets and had a crier to make it known to the multitude. Our Lord said of them the ominous words: "Amen, amen, they have received their reward!"[70] This hunger for praise and publicity makes people do, not merely childish and ridiculous things, but things mean and disgraceful.

Some people would almost sell their souls for a higher place at a banquet table or for a chairman's seat at a committee meeting. Some people will persistently angle for praise so that their reluctant and half-mocking neighbors will finally give it to get rid of them. Some will lie and exaggerate about their fictitious achievements to gather fraudulent congratulations. Some will calumniate and lie about others, or at least unduly belittle them, so that they themselves may stand out as noble heroes above the vulgar herd.

Deeds done for the sole purpose of gaining the approval and esteem of men, although perchance good deeds in themselves, lose all merit before God. The honor they get from men is their payment, and no further payment is due. Perhaps we guard against

---

[70] Matt. 6:2.

such exclusive and complete vitiation of our virtuous acts, but it is difficult to prevent a mixture of motives: half vanity, half good intention. We must be watchful and examine ourselves.

Honor, if merited and unsought, is no evil, but the secret desire for public acknowledgment may, so to say, devour all or nearly all the inner goodness and merits of so many of our actions. A Christian's attitude toward honors should rather be that of a shrinking, nay, a running away from them, as Christ ran away from the attempts to make Him king. Surely we Christians can afford to wait for our glorification in Heaven. God will give us our due before the angels and the blessed of His heavenly court. There our title and true distinction will be proclaimed. It seems paltry to trouble much about the honors we may gather from our fellowmen. All the world's glory is but a fleeting, flimsy thing.

Part Four

Practice virtue

⁀

Chapter Twenty-Four

Put on our Lord Jesus Christ

The Bible, especially the New Testament, has many quaint expressions that cannot but puzzle first hearers. The expression of St. Paul is a case in point. "Brethren, put ye on the Lord Jesus Christ."[71] What does that mean?

How can anyone put on our Lord and be clothed with Him as with a garment? Yet St. Paul repeats the statement elsewhere and says, "As many of you as were baptized in Christ, have put on Christ."[72] We might say that St. Paul had in mind the donning of a livery of a king, or the investing with the robe of knighthood, which throws a dignity and a glory around a person far beyond his own acquirements or claims, and which makes him a sharer of the majesty of his Sovereign and involves corresponding duties. If a king should give to his subject his own royal mantle to wear, it would mean the bestowal of some sort of kingliness, a willing acknowledgment of intimacy, and well-nigh equality.

Christ allowed us to put Him on, so to unite ourselves to Him, that He might become our adornment and our splendor. Since we

[71] Rom. 13:14.
[72] Gal. 3:27.

are the adopted children of God, the only-begotten Son of God decided to give us some of the style and state of His own Royal House.

According to Christ's parable, when the Prodigal Son returned, the Father said, "Bring forth quickly the first robe and put it on him, and put a ring on his hand and shoes on his feet,"[73] so that he should be becomingly clad and not be put to shame when compared with the other brother, who had never left his father's house. So likewise did the heavenly Father do with prodigal mankind when His elder, eternal Son, who was always with Him and to whom, before all ages, He had said, "All I have is Thine!" had brought His lost brethren back to His Father's house at the price of His own Blood, for the only-begotten Son has no envy of His humble human brothers, as the elder son in the parable had.

We can read, however, in Holy Scripture a much deeper meaning still. A garment is something that covers and envelops, warms and protects. Be it an adornment or not, it is something necessary and intimate and personal to us, something that clings to us and surrounds and encompasses us. In this sense, our Lord ought to be our vesture, and we must be clothed with Him.

Everyone has heard the homely expression about a person being very fond of another: "Oh, he is wrapped up in her." It means that his personality is almost merged into that of the other, that in a sense, he has lost his self in the self of the other. So ought a Christian to be wrapped up in Christ and lose himself in Him.

There are so many of us, who, among a number of titles, occupations, and claims, are also Christians. If asked whether we acknowledge Christ, the answer would be in the affirmative: "Oh, quite, of course," but our perfunctory reply would hardly suggest that He is our bosom friend and that all our waking thoughts are occupied with Him.

[73] Luke 15:22.

We are certainly no Jonathan to our David. Christ may keep His arms outstretched upon the Cross, ready for our embrace, but we prefer to keep a respectful distance and have no very urgent desire to feel our heart throb against His and His against ours. Our religion is a very cool affair; we are certainly not wrapped up in it.

Yet Christianity is not merely the keeping of a respectable code of conduct. Christianity is Christ. To live as a Christian is to live in union with Christ. The perfection of Christianity is the love of Christ; a loveless Christianity is a false Christianity. Many will assent to this in the sense that Christians must love their neighbors, but not in the sense that they must love Christ.

Well known is the old story of the respectable Jew, Moses Isaacs, who claimed that he was as good a Christian as anyone, for he led a decent life. If Christianity was only a "respectable" life, Moses Isaacs was right, but then Christ need never have come, and the Incarnation was much ado about nothing.

To be a Christian means to put on Christ, to have Him as our bosom Friend, to have Him as our most beloved Brother, to be wrapped up in Him, to cherish Him in all our thoughts, to knit our lives with His, so that His will is ours, His merest wish our law. To be a Christian means consciously, deliberately to live not B.C., but A.D.

We Christians are not glorified Jews or pagans. We live in the light of the truth that the Word, who is God, became flesh and forever dwells among us, to be the Lover as well as the Savior of souls.

☞

Chapter Twenty-Five

Conduct yourself as a child of God

When people disapprove of their neighbors' behavior, they often say, "It is not gentlemanly" or "It is not ladylike," and it is taken to be a sharp rebuke when they say to us, "You are not a gentleman" or "You are not a lady." The world has its code of honor and courtesy, and it boycotts those who do not observe it. It calls them "impossible people" and banishes them from good society.

It must be admitted that "a perfect gentleman," in the sense of the world, is a delightful person. But God's gentleman is a beautiful character in a higher sense, and with a deeper meaning than that of social refinements, for it is based on more than outward behavior. It is based on an inward likeness to Christ — Christlikeness in man's soul.

St. Paul gives us a description of God's gentleman: "Brethren, since ye are the elect of God, holy and beloved, put ye on the tenderness of mercy, benignity, humility, modesty, patience."[74] St. Paul means, "Since from all eternity God has chosen you to be His holy ones, His beloved ones, behave not as the Devil's men, callous, unkind, haughty, boastful, and irritable. Put off the old man,

[74] Cf. Col. 3:12.

and put on the garment of Christ. You are God's gentlemen now, and gentleness is typical of one who follows Jesus, who said, 'Learn from me, that I am meek and humble of heart.' "

Now, there are Christians who style themselves rough diamonds. Of their roughness there can be no doubt, but their diamond-nature is not so apparent, except perhaps in this: that they are hard on their fellowmen and know how to drive a hard bargain. They lack the tenderness of Christ.

A man can be tender without being sloppy; a woman can be tender without being sentimental. Christian tenderness is the spontaneous outcome of profound pity, the manifestation of a merciful heart. Even a worldly person can adopt a thin veneer of courtesy and sympathy. For the Christian, the matter lies much deeper. It is based on unselfishness akin to that immense pity which brought Christ to the Cross, so that by His death He might heal the wounds, sufferings, and sorrows of His brethren. It begets that benignity of which the apostle speaks, that kindliness without offensive condescension, which comes from realizing that we men are all equal in the sight of Heaven and that we all equally need the grace and the pardon of God.

Fellow sinners should bear with one another, for they are all in the same plight; God has to bear with them. A Christian is a man who has at least some idea of the awesome holiness of God and what that dread sanctity demands from creatures.

Even when meeting sinners, he does not show the whites of his eyes, for he knows too well that, but for the grace of God, he might be worse than they. The world tramples on a man who has fallen; the Christian, in affectionate simplicity, stoops to pick him up. He applies the world's own proverb "Don't kick a man when he is down" even to those who are not only down on their luck, but down in sin and degradation.

The Christlike man does not go through the world blustering and blundering, elbowing his neighbors out of the way to get the best bits of the world's banquet or to reach the highest seat. He knows something at least of the modesty of Christ, who was satisfied with a carpenter's wage and sought no entrance into the palaces of the great.

The true Christian is too much of a gentleman to be in an unseemly hurry. He knows how to possess his soul in patience and not, by his temper, embitter the lives of his fellows or make his household a home of strife. Being and knowing himself to be one of God's elect, holy and beloved, to use scriptural terms, he feels it does not befit him to play the bully and behave boorishly just because things do not go to his liking.

A raging mouth and a venomous look spoil the features of a person who claims to be brother or sister to Christ.

> *Give us then, Jesus, mercy, mildness,*
> *lowliness, modesty, and patience.*
> *Imprint on our souls the virtue of gentleness,*
> *and teach us the manners fit for*
> *the chosen and beloved of God.*

Chapter Twenty-Six

Pattern your heart on Christ's

On a thousand pictures and statues we see our Lord pointing to the Sacred Heart on His breast. Naturally we first regard it as a manifestation of His own divine love, but soon we also hear the words "Learn from me,"[75] and we realize that it is the pattern of what a human heart should be and that so often we fall short of that divine ideal.

We may comfort ourselves with the excuse that we are honest, just, and straightforward, that we are clean, chaste, and religious, but, if truth were told, we could not deny that we act toward our neighbor most heartlessly. In fact, from some of our words and deeds, it might seem as if we had no heart at all. It is not that we expressly seek to hurt others, or take a delight in it, but we just do not care whether we do or not.

Regard for other people's feelings is not our strong point. If we are going to make our way in the world, we cannot afford to be sentimental, we say. We almost boast that we are rough-and-ready, that we speak the truth and shame the Devil; if other folks do not like it, well, they must lump it. If they want to be touchy, well, let

<hr>

[75] Matt. 11:29.

them; we cannot be bothered. No cook can make omelets without breaking eggs.

And so in life we have smashed our way through, regardless and indifferent to having left many a sore and wounded heart, many an embittered, broken heart behind. We did not do it of set purpose, or with direct malice; so much may be conceded. We seldom thought whether our behavior would bring sorrow or suffering to others, or, if we happened to think of it, we shrugged our shoulders and forgot it a moment afterward. We are overbearing; we must have our way. Maybe we are strictly just and respect the letter of the law, but we understand only force and compulsion; whether this brings an agony of pain to our neighbor and fills his eyes with tears little concerns us. We have learned no meekness from the Heart of Jesus.

Incredulous, we smile at the beatitude "The meek shall possess the earth";[76] we do not believe it. We believe in being hard; we scoff at the idea of being soft. Instead of copying the tenderness of our Lord, we have become more like the pagans of whom holy Scripture says that they are "without affection."[77] An affectionate man is an unselfish man; his neighbor's sorrow or joy is as his own. His heart feels for others, even as Jesus' Heart feels for us, even though we are sinners and have done Him to death.

A second reason for our heartlessness lies in our pride. A proud person finds it hard to love. In all love, there must be some humility. It is almost proverbial that lovers are apt to make fools of themselves. O blessed divine folly that brought Jesus to the Cross and laid His Sacred Heart open to the lance of the soldier on Golgotha!

Pride means isolation, lonesomeness, and hardness of heart. Pride is the death of all real tenderness, for tenderness means

[76] Ps. 36:11 (RSV = Ps. 37:11); Matt. 5:4.
[77] Rom. 1:31.

warmth of soul, and pride freezes the human soul until it becomes stark and cold, without feeling, and bereft of life. When a proud person begins to love, at once a struggle begins within, and until his haughtiness is broken, love cannot triumph. Christ humbled Himself unto death, yea, unto the death of the Cross, and thus proved Himself the Lover of men and could forever show His pierced Heart as token of God's love. Thereby He obtained the right to give us a new command: "That you love one another, as I also have loved you."[78]

We must, then, learn from Him to be meek and humble of heart. Root out selfishness and pride, and the wretched heartlessness that now mars and disfigures the interchange between man and man will disappear. A glow of friendliness, of care and mutual consideration will soon illumine and warm the earth. The ice of unconcern, the frost of cold indifference to one another will soon melt, and men will begin to behave as what they are: brothers to one another. The hearts of men will begin to resemble the Heart of Christ, for it is He who has shamed us into caring for the brethren when He allowed the centurion to open His side and lay bare the Heart of God made man.

To every act of human love directed to Him, the Redeemer will answer, "If you love me, love one another. Let your hearts throb in unison with mine, for I loved and love you all with a love without end."

[78] John 15:12.

Chapter Twenty-Seven

⌒

Strive to live the Beatitudes

The world's eight beatitudes differ greatly from those of Christ.[79] "Lucky are the rich, for they shall be as kings on earth. Lucky are the pushy, for they shall possess the land. Lucky are the merry, for they need ask no one for comfort. Lucky are they who hunger and thirst only for worldly success, for they are likely to have their fill. Lucky are the ruthless, for they are not hampered by regard for other people's feelings. Lucky are the careless about cleanness of heart, for they can enjoy the beauties of sense. Lucky are those who hold more than their own in the fight for goods, for they shall be called children of the world. Lucky are they who escape defeat in fiercest competition, for they shall be as kings here on earth."

We all have to choose between the two sets of beatitudes. Those of the world seem so sensible; those of Christ are stern. Those of the world sound so delightful; those of Christ sound so doleful, at least on first hearing. There are just two things in favor of the Beatitudes of Christ.

Christ's blessings go deeper than those of the world, and they are more lasting. Note that the world does not even dare to speak

[79] Matt. 5:3-11.

of "blessings." The world, by a sort of instinct, avoids saying, "Blessed is the man," but prefers saying, "Lucky is the man." Now, luck is something external and almost alien to a man. Luck is not really part of a man; it comes to him from without and, therefore, there is an element of uncertainty about it. The promised boon may never come, and even if it does, it may not make you happy.

A man who is suddenly rich by winning a sweepstakes may be called "lucky," but whether he will be happy is quite another question. Inward rest and contentment, joy of soul and the grace of God are not things that the world can promise. Poverty, meekness, mourning, hunger and thirst, pity, purity, peacefulness, and persecution seem hard conditions for blessing, were it not that it is a divine blessing and, pervading the whole man, fills him with unspeakable happiness, a happiness independent of chance and fortune, a happiness that penetrates deeper than the surface jollity, the shallow laughter, and the passing amusement of the worldling.

Those who inherit the blessings of Christ seem to be immersed by God deep into the still sea of His own divine tranquility, a joy that is beyond change and variation. Their gaze becomes steady, their features calm. No twitching lips betray inward unrest; no jerky gesture or feeble gait betrays uncertainty of purpose.

The beatitude of Christ has descended on the true Christian, and he possesses himself in peace. He is happier even in this life than the world could make him if he followed its doubtful recipes for human happiness.

Besides being deeper, Christ's blessings last longer. Death makes short work of all that the world can offer, whereas death means the complete fulfillment of all that Christ has promised.

It was right and just that the Church should have chosen the proclamation of the eight Beatitudes as the Gospel for the Feast of All Saints. That vast multitude, which no one can number, is placed before our eyes, so that we may rejoice with those who have obtained eternal blessedness by trusting here on earth in the charter of Christ's kingdom and so that we may imitate their example and beg their intercession that we also may persevere until the end.

The saints thought it wise while on earth to be poor in spirit and meek in speech and conduct. They bore sorrows well for the sake of God's consolation. Their greatest striving, their craving like hunger and thirst was for God's sanctifying grace, and God gave unto them their fill. They showed mercy to others as they hoped to receive mercy from God. They kept themselves chaste and pure, unstained in this present wicked world, in the hope that one day they might see God face-to-face. They loved peace more than war and even suffered persecution without a murmur, knowing well that their treasures were laid up in Heaven.[80]

Therefore have they now entered into eternal rest, and perpetual light shines upon them. They move in a realm of bliss never ending, for God has wiped the tears from their eyes. For them, mourning, crying, or sorrow shall be no more, for God has made all things new. Eye has not seen, ear has not heard, neither has it entered into the heart of man here on earth what God has prepared in Heaven for those who, out of love for Him, trusted in the eight Beatitudes of Christ while they were still passing through mortal life.[81]

Intercede for us,
you brethren and sisters
who stand in safety around
the throne of Christ above,
so that we may join your happy throng
and share our triumph in the
blessedness of life everlasting.

[80] Cf. Matt. 6:20.
[81] Cf. 1 Cor. 2:9.

Chapter Twenty-Eight

~

Be cheerful

We are apt to look a little disapprovingly on a person who always sees things with rose-colored glasses and never seems to realize the gravity of the situation. In a sense we are right.

There are persons who can never be serious, who treat everything as if it were a joke and can never summon up sufficient earnestness to decide important issues. There is a lightheartedness that is akin to lightheadedness, and we have all heard of the perpetual grin on the face of the idiot. There is a smile that is only a token of indifference or a proof of laziness and lack of care. Granting all this, we must acknowledge that it is a valuable and lovable virtue to be lighthearted and a gift of God to be able to see things on earth with rose-colored glasses.

Pessimism is not from God. Saints do not pass through life with a scowl on their faces. There is a telling New Testament text: "God loveth a cheerful giver."[82] Cheerfulness is an act of worship toward God, an act of kindness toward our neighbor, and a healthy exercise for our own soul. To turn a smiling face toward Heaven is to praise God and to give Him thanks because He is good. To

---

[82] 2 Cor. 9:7.

stroke away the frown from our forehead and to look around us with kindly, merry eyes, for the sake of our Father in Heaven, who does not like to see sullen, sulky faces, is a true and noble act of religion.

If a guest in our house moped about the premises with downcast looks and a sour mouth, a picture of groaning misery, we would not like it. We are guests in God's universe, and God is our Host. He expects us to say, "Thank You," not with a moan and a sob, our features belying our words, but with a bright glance and blithe lips. To do so is a real act of homage and is frequently more meritorious than the recital of a long psalm of gloom and misery.

But there is so much sorrow and pain in the world! So there is, but there is also much deep innocent happiness in this world, and if we believe in God and serve Him, eternal happiness awaits us, whereas pain and sorrow shall forever pass away. In the strength of that faith, we should give glory to God, from whom all good things come.

Cheerfulness is an act of kindness toward our neighbor. Happiness is happily contagious; gloom acts like a dangerous infection. Miserable people spread misery around them. Think of a nursery. When one baby starts crying, soon the whole multitude follows suit. Adults are not very different. Let someone start a gloomy conversation, and soon the whole company is plunged into sadness. Sometimes not even a word need be said; the mere presence of a pessimist, with his drawn features, his dull eyes, his sinking mouth, his only half-suppressed sigh, stops merry laughter and casts a shadow over a happy party, and he is an evil genius who has stolen the smiles from their faces.

There are pessimists who are positively angry because other people are happy. They envy them their very happiness. They argue that people ought to be unhappy. They rest not until other people also are wretched and unhappy; only then with a gloomy satisfaction do they go their way.

On the other hand, what a blessing are those who spread sunshine wherever they go! Personally they may have reasons for grief, but they hide it, lest they should darken the day for their neighbor. They would think it cruel to intrude their grief on others; with noble heroism, they try to keep a smiling face through it all. Often in a household there is one such blithe spirit, who is a blessing to all the family and source of joy in the home. Such people are the benefactors of mankind, true disciples of Him who said, "Be ye of good cheer, little ones; I have overcome the world."[83]

Cheerfulness is a healthy exercise for our own soul. Too much sadness weakens the will. To put a check on moodiness may be difficult, but it is an invigorating practice. People who weakly and feebly give way to continual depression are like folk living in a cellar; they become pale and anemic, frail and sickly. They ought to shake off their depression and come out into the open to see that the sun is still in the sky. This may cost a momentary self-conquest, a momentary strong exertion, but God asks it of them for the health of their soul.

More souls are lost by despondency than by almost any other spiritual disease. Hence, Christ says to us, "When you fast, be not as the hypocrites, sad . . . but thou, when thou fastest, anoint thy head and wash thy face . . . and thy Father who seeth in secret will repay thee."[84]

[83] Cf. John 16:33.
[84] Matt. 6:16-18.

Part Five

Fight sin

Chapter Twenty-Nine

༄

Form your conscience

"The hour cometh, that whosoever killeth you will think that he doth a service to God," says the Gospel.[85] This is surely the most appalling instance of false conscience that can be imagined. Murder of innocent servants of God to be thought a service to Him! Yet our Lord said well, "The hour cometh," for it was not to be long before Saul of Tarsus "was breathing out threatenings and slaughter against the disciples of the Lord"[86] and made himself believe that he was doing God's will thereby.

The danger of a false conscience exists for all of us. People thoroughly wicked and depraved do evil, fully intending the evil. Many do evil with an uneasy conscience, half-aware of the evil they do and hoping God will forgive it. But there are also many who, at the time of the deed, have persuaded themselves that they are doing right, although, in fact, they are wrong, often grievously wrong. In such a case, a man might say, "No harm is done. God judges a man according to his conscience at the time." This would be so if a man were never responsible for his own conscience, but this is not so.

---

[85] John 16:2.
[86] Acts 9:1.

Ten Minutes a Day to Heaven

A man may be deeply guilty of his false conscience. I heard of a Catholic young fellow who had gone to fight for the Communists in Spain during the Spanish Civil War. Quite possibly he imagined that he was doing a fine thing, but the record of the fellow's conduct was such, his scoffing neglect of Church and sacraments such, that his ghastly perversion of conscience was not just an innocent mistake for which he was not responsible.

A man, to a large extent, makes his own conscience, either by yielding to the grace of God or by listening to the whispers of the Devil. There is such a thing as training a conscience for good or for evil. Passion darkens conscience. A man who acts in passion has only himself to blame if he does things that, in bitterness of soul, he later recognizes as utterly wrong and unjustified. Fierce emotion is usually a dangerous counselor. A man who wants a sound verdict about what is allowed or disallowed had better cool down and calm down first, and give himself time for long consideration in matters of grave import.

A homely saying has much truth: Sleep on it first. Give it a day before you decide.

A second source of a false conscience is secret self-interest. We are ourselves involved in the case before us. We are not deciding an abstract point or something that affects only strangers. Regarding others, our judgment may be keen and correct; indeed, we are usually very sharp and clear when we give our opinion on what others ought to do. But when our own advantage or disadvantage comes into play, our view of the case becomes colored and blurred. We suddenly see reasons for a line of conduct that would seem ludicrous to us if another man brought them forward. We start arguing with ourselves and almost like a shrewd, unscrupulous lawyer, we argue ourselves into a certain position. Then we still any murmuring that is about to arise from our innermost selves, and we boldly proceed on what we are pleased to call "our conscience." All the time God, who searches the inner man, "the reins and the heart,"[87] condemns our false conscience, for we have faked it for ourselves.

A third most fruitful source of error is our self-sufficiency and pride. Theoretically, of course, we allow that we are fallible and that our conscience may be mistaken, but in practice we vehemently resent that anyone should call into question our judgment about our own behavior.

"I stand or fall by my own conscience," we haughtily say. "It is impertinent to question a man's conscience." Quite true. A man must ultimately follow his conscience if, after much humble prayer and after duly taking counsel, he comes to his final conclusion that God wants him to do or not to do something, but a careless casual opinion arrived at without prayer, without any asking of advice, cannot be dubbed conscience.

Christ has left His Church as the supernatural counselor of the children of God. Her priests, especially in the tribunal of Penance, are God's officials and ministers, whose judgment is likely to be unbiased and prudent and safely to be followed. If in a grave matter of conscience, when common sense would suggest extreme care, we rush forward because we have a notion that this is right, or that without a supplication to the Holy Spirit, the Spirit of Truth, without a word with a priest or a wise friend, we may not be guiltless in our error of judgment or sadly crooked conscience.

Conscience is a tender thing; with rough handling it can be twisted into monstrous shapes. There is history enough to prove it!

[87] Cf. Ps. 7:10 (RSV = Ps. 7:9).

Chapter Thirty

⌒

Do not make excuses for your sins

The Devil, the world, and the flesh combine in a hideous conspiracy to hide from men the enormity of sin. The facts are that God, who in His divine nature cannot suffer, took our human nature, so that as man He might suffer agony and die to atone for the sins of man. The appalling greatness of sin is made manifest in the mangled, tortured dead body of God upon the Cross. God made Himself a victim and a sacrifice unto His divine holiness for the undoing of man's sin, so that thus man might at last believe that sin was no slight thing, no trifling evil in the sight of God. Man is brought up suddenly and sharply to face the Cross on Golgotha to acknowledge the dread reality of sin.

The wretched process of deception is ever going on to prevent man from seeing the truth. "The Devil deceived me, and I ate," said the first sinner,[88] and so have all sinners said since, but, oh, the pity, after the sin is done, and so often after the chance of repentance is gone. Before the sin is committed, the Devil will smirk and smile and say in soft tones, "There is no serious harm in it. You will enjoy it. Maybe God threatens dire things, but He only

[88] Cf. Gen. 3:13.

half-means it, and pardon is easily procured." And man, silly as he is, believes it, or rather, wants to believe it. He beguiles himself and does the accursed thing, unless in time he remembers the Cross and is frightened by the wounds, the agony, and the death of Christ. These tell him that sin is not just jest and fun for God, a paltry thing easily overlooked.

The world keeps up the lie that the Devil began. They say, "It is the verdict of modern science!" Psychology, they claim, has explained the mechanism of the human will. It is all the outcome of inhibitions and complexes, heredity and instinctive impulses, automatic reactions, accidents in babyhood, and whatnot.

When a man's behavior is what they style "antisocial," it is like the measles; it is a disease that science must cure, but whatever you do, do not mention sin to him. Science knows nothing of sin; it is only some sort of "behaviorism."

The more honest person or, to put it better, the less hypocritical person may perchance not invoke the verdict of science. They will say straight out, "Everyone is doing it; there cannot be much harm in it. They think nothing of it. Why should you be singular and make such a fuss? The priests are like a flock of black crows, always cawing about crime and sin. Leave them, and follow the merry crowd. God is not an ogre. God is too big to mind the peccadilloes of men. Even if the thing is not quite correct, God is good and easily forgives."

This lie has deceived many a man, unless indeed he swiftly turned his gaze to Calvary and there saw the truth. The head crowned with thorns, the lips parched with thirst, the features bedraggled with spittle and dirt, the body torn by the scourges, and the hands and feet nailed to the wood tell a different tale of what God thinks of sin. Human deeds that cry for such atonement are not quite the pardonable jokes that the world tries to make out. There must be a mystery of iniquity; there must be a depth of evil in what man, self-blinded to God's holiness, so often, so glibly, so boastfully perpetrates in scornful merriment at God's easy mercy.

There is a third lie, which, apart from the Devil and the world, we are trying again and again to make ourselves believe: "I am weak. I cannot really help it; my passions run away with me. After all, God Himself has given me my nature, and He will understand. He cannot be hard on me. My sins are sins not of malice, but of frailty. The spirit is willing, but the flesh is weak. It is really only my body, not my soul that sins."

So argues a man with himself, and sometimes almost cajoles himself that there is not much amiss with him, and that, in any case, there is easy forgiveness for him, even though he has led a sinful life.

But when he studies his crucifix, sterner and truer thoughts come to him. When he thinks of Christ's Passion and Christ's agony in the garden, of Christ's threefold fall under the Cross to atone for the cowardly surrender of the sinner to his lower nature and the yielding to his baser instinct, the cold truth dawns upon him that Christ had to suffer to raise and redeem that nature which man so shamefully degrades.

Let us, therefore, look into ourselves and let the wounds of Christ speak to our soul and rouse in us a sentiment of sorrow for past sins and a determination not to make light of sin again. May a spirit of atonement pervade us in accepting the atonement of the Cross in order that one day we may accept the glory of the Resurrection.

Chapter Thirty-One

⌒

Avoid occasions of sin

It seems beyond doubt that the majority of sins that men commit are not done after long planning and scheming with malice afore-thought. They are more or less sudden falls in temptation; men seem rushed into them under the impulse of the moment. Inveter-ate sinners after years of sinning may think out their sin long be-forehand, but most of us sin because we forget St. Paul's warning: "He that stands, let him take heed lest he fall."[89]

Are we therefore guiltless? No! Possibly, in the actual deed, our guilt was lessened by the blinding power of passion, be it covet-ousness, impurity, or anger, but we were guilty, for the temptation itself was our doing; we ran into it, heedlessly, wantonly, presump-tuously. There was that person whom we instinctively strongly disliked. We saw an opportunity of going and telling him off, as the expression runs. We intended not to lose our temper, only to give him the truth, the unvarnished truth — for his own benefit, of course. We come away after a vehement quarrel, after blows, perhaps, enemies for life; we started a family feud that may last for generations, and we are seething with hate.

[89] 1 Cor. 10:12.

Are we guiltless because we saw red and we did not know what we were saying or doing? Certainly not. We went to meet temptation and fell into it; the feeble resolution not to lose our temper was only a sop to quiet our conscience.

There was that person who, we felt, had a fatal attraction for us, who seemed to bewitch us and charm us, whose picture we could scarcely drive from our imagination and whose presence sent us off our balance. We went to see him or her on some flimsy pretext. We said to ourselves, "Of course I won't do any wrong!" But we came back from our visit with our conscience soiled, our honor lost, and our soul in sin. Are we guiltless? Certainly not. The plea that we lost control of ourselves and could not help it, that the temptation was too strong — that plea will not avail, for we sought the temptation and found it. It gripped us and pulled us down. The guilt and the shame are on our soul.

There was that person with the careless habit of leaving cash lying around and not closing the drawers of his bureau. We went to his room, not to take anything, of course, but only just to see how careless he could be. We left his room with his money in our pocket. We excuse ourselves by saying that we cannot understand how we came to do it; some irresistible impulse drove us to take it. Are we guiltless? Indeed we are not. The demon of covetousness seduced us into that room just to gloat over that money, knowing quite well that it would be easy to make us close our fist over it. Our sin was to risk it.

No one has any right to take risks in matters of eternal import. Gaining Heaven is not a game, nor is Hell to be escaped by a mere toss-up. Let him who stands take heed lest he fall. Taking heed means praying against the time of temptation. No one can in the long run resist serious temptations without praying, and not only at the very instant of the attack, but steadily and perseveringly before it. It is not without reason that our Lord taught the final petition of the Our Father. No one can in the long run resist temptations unless he is determined to flee them and not to dally and play with them. The Devil is not a suitable play-fellow. He cheats at cards. He pretends that you have a strong hand and are sure to win, but you will lose.

⌒

Chapter Thirty-Two

Remember that God sees all that you do

God dwells in the world and is within all things, great and small. Or rather, we should say, the world is in God, for God's infinite mind and will wraps it around, and pierces it through and through from end to end, and goes beyond. Invisible to us though He be, He envelops, embraces, and holds us. He is present in our inmost soul, and in the depth of our being He is to be found. He is nearer to us than all things else, and no created thing is closer to us than He.

When as little children we were asked the seemingly simple question "Where is God?" our young voices merrily piped out, "God is everywhere," and we thought ourselves clever in knowing the answer. When as old men or women we repeat to ourselves, "God is everywhere," we tremble at the greatness of the truth, and the appalling nearness of the majesty overcomes us.

God has seen us ever. He has listened to us always. He read our most hidden thoughts as if they were an open book. "I am a God close at hand and not a God afar off," saith the Lord.[90] "In Him we live, we move and have our being," saith the Scriptures.[91]

[90] Cf. Jer. 23:23.
[91] Acts 17:28.

As the bird is in the air, as the fishes are in the sea, so are we in God, and we cannot escape from the wideness of His Heaven, or go beyond the ocean of His being. We are enclosed in Him, even though there are no boundaries to His glory.

Three thousand years ago, the psalmist asked the question to which there is no answer: "Whither shall I go from Thy spirit, or whither shall I flee from Thy face? If I ascend into Heaven, Thou art there; if I descend into hell, Thou art present. If I take my wings early in the dawn and dwell in the uttermost parts of the sea, even there also shall Thy hand lead me and Thy right hand shall hold me. And I said: Perhaps darkness shall cover me; and night shall be my light in my pleasures, but darkness is not dark unto Thee, and night is light as the day. Darkness and light are alike unto Thee."[92]

If only we could keep the presence of God in mind and always consciously "walk before His face,"[93] to use a biblical phrase, we would surely be on the road to Heaven. But we forget. Why do we forget? Because all the silly trifles of this world totally absorb our attention. We do not give ourselves time to think.

Suppose a man once a day stood still, be it but for one minute, and deliberately placed himself mentally in the presence of God: would not that man make progress in the science of the saints, for what are saints? They are people who in all their thoughts, words, and deeds keep God in mind; people who always feel the eyes of God upon them, who always realize that God is listening, that God is reading their thoughts — in other words, that they can never get away from God. No sane person would deny that God is everywhere, but too many persons act as if God were far away, a distant potentate, an absentee ruler, living in unknown realms beyond. The thought of God's presence ought to be the strongest

[92] Ps. 138:7-12 (RSV = Ps. 139:7-12).
[93] Cf. Gen. 17:1.

check in time of temptation and the strongest urge to do good throughout life.

It is the strongest check in temptation, for who would sin while he said to himself, "God is looking at me. God stands in front of me and watches me. God is reading the evil intent in my heart"? Instinctively the sinner hides, after the example of the first sinner, of whom it stands written: "Adam and his wife hid themselves from the face of the Lord God amidst the trees of Paradise."[94]

Idle attempt! They were too late. They should have thought earlier of the face of the Lord their God, and the tempter would not have deceived them.

An ancient symbol of the Blessed Trinity is a triangle with an open eye within it. It would not be a bad idea for some of us to fix such an emblem on the wall of our room and write under it, "God sees me!" Such a symbol would strike terror in us when we are inclined to sin; it would cheer us in time of sorrow and fill us with joy in doing good. Our good actions might never be noticed by men, our good intentions might be misunderstood and misinterpreted even by friends, but that friendly eye sees all and knows all.

[94] Gen. 3:8.

⌒

Chapter Thirty-Three

Atone for your sins

We often pray for the faithful departed. What is less often done is to ask ourselves what these souls in Purgatory would say to us if they were allowed by God to reappear among us and give us a few words of advice. As a matter of fact, God but very rarely permits the reappearance of the dead among the living. Sometimes, indeed, a soul in Purgatory gives some sign, either to ask for prayers or to warn those whom they loved on earth, but this happens exceedingly seldom.

For all that, our Faith does readily suggest to us what sort of counsel our departed loved ones would give us, were they for a few moments to return again in our family circle. Say, then, someone near and dear to us — a father or mother, wife or child, brother or friend — came again and spoke to us. What would they say?

"I am saved indeed and destined for Heaven, but I am in the realm of sorrow and waiting, in the land of twilight and exile, in a region of wandering and solitude. I am in an agony of longing for my God, but in bitter pain am I being purified until I am allowed in His presence. Take warning from me! I am where I am on account of two things: during my lifetime, I offended my God and I repented. My repentance was true, but it was very imperfect.

"My repentance was true, I confessed, and by God's grace, my guilt was forgiven and the black deformity of my soul was gone, but I was too easily satisfied. Heaven was open again and the threat of Hell removed; it was enough for me. I did not trouble overmuch to pay the debt owing to the holiness and justice of God. I rejoiced indeed in God's mercy that forgave me, but I gave little heed to the demands of divine righteousness. I had been to Confession and had been duly absolved; all seemed well, and there was nothing more to be done. Even after a very serious fault, the priest gave me a few Rosaries or litanies to say. I said them, of course, correctly, but not with much fervor. I did not continue works of penance. I never really paid my debt to God for forgiven sin. I grudged Him any act of voluntary mortification. I did not even bear patiently the common difficulties of life, and now I must pay the last penny in spiritual pain.

"What I might have freely offered to the mercy of God and thus increased its value, I must now offer to the inexorable holiness of His infinite majesty. Even more than this: besides my forgiven grievous faults that cried for penance, there are a thousand lesser failings, so-called venial sins. I made little of them, and they added up to an enormous number. I elicited no act of sorrow for them. I thought them trifles. I forgot all about them. If I remembered them, I took them lightly and smiled, saying to myself that I was only human and that other people were as bad as I and worse. They lost their temper, were uncharitable, told untruths, were not straight and honest in small matters, and had as many peccadilloes as I. Thus I comforted myself and made myself believe that God would not mind such things very much.

"God is merciful, said I, as if being merciful meant being soft and easy-going and slovenly, overlooking things in whimsical fashion or because He cannot be bothered. But I found that the fierce scorching light of the awful holiness of God is not a thing to be played with. On earth I treated many matters as a joke, but I found that God does not understand such jokes. I could not carry off things so easily before God's throne as I passed them off during my earthly life with a smile or a shrug of the shoulders.

"Take warning from me! God indeed is infinitely good, and I always lovingly adore Him, but the majesty of God is great. His love is not that of a simpleton without the strength of character to know the holy wrath of justice."

In such a way, a soul in Purgatory would surely speak to his former loved ones on earth.

Maybe our prayers have already opened the gates of Heaven for some who were once our relatives or friends on this side of the grave, but others surely remain who have not finished their weary waiting for the sight of God face-to-face. Both those already in Heaven and those destined to get to Heaven, would, as far as their warning went, use the same language to us.

Be wise in time! Before death, every act of voluntary penance, every patient submission to the hardships of life is like paying our debt with gold. After death, it is only silver, and the debt will take long in paying.

Now it is gold, for we can still merit; after death comes the night in which no one can work, but only suffer to satisfy the justice of God.

Chapter Thirty-Four

⌒

Practice self-denial

"Many things are lawful, but not all things are expedient."[95] Lent is the time for voluntary abstinence from lawful things, but such abstinence should not be limited to Lent; it is a principle that pervades the life of every true Christian.

A man who always insists on his right — however trifling — a man who wants the utmost enjoyment out of life is not a true Christian. He forgets the fact of the Fall. He forgets the duty of penitence. He forgets that a religion that costs nothing is worth nothing.

We are a weak and fallen race. Our character wants stiffening and strengthening. Hardships well borne are the best means of steeling ourselves against the allurements of unlawful joys. A man might plead that life for him is hard enough and he needs not seek extra hardships. In a few cases, this is no doubt true. Such a man might show heroic constancy and might train his will to admirable strength by carrying his burden without murmuring, without going in quest of more painful sacrifices. But in many cases, perhaps most, it is not so.

[95] Cf. 1 Cor. 6:12.

Usually there is a large margin of possible and lawful pleasures a man might do without and yet not injure mind or body by excessive mortification. If we have trained ourselves to forgo harmless pleasures from time to time, if we have taken ourselves in hand and deliberately exercised control, for the sake of being master of ourselves, if we have set a sweet aside, or, so to say, almost taken it out of our mouth, not because there was any sin in it, but because we did not want to be slave to our desires, we have gained a victory, which is the forecast of many triumphs in times of temptation.

If we are soft and indulgent, if the moment we fancy a thing, we simply must have it, if we are accustomed never to say no to ourselves, then we fall an easy prey to sinful passions. We have not got the stamina to resist. Our spiritual muscles are flabby. We have never really struggled with ourselves, and when the real serious battle is upon us, we are overthrown almost before we have struck a blow. We have always given in to ourselves. Now we are asked to refuse ourselves something. This time we must not yield to our inclination, but we have always yielded before. In consequence, we make only some feeble gestures, but end by surrendering. That is the secret of many a moral disaster: a soft, self-indulgent life without any mortification.

Unmortified people forget the duty of penitence. Were we all spotless saints and had never sinned, we might make some plea that we had a right to enjoy anything that came along and seek for anything that might give us pleasure. But is it seemly that we, who have so often stolen unlawful pleasures against the law of God, should never offer in reparation to do without something that took our fancy? Quite true: God has forgiven us, the guilt of our sin has gone, but this is scarcely a reason for forgetting the holiness and justice of God, as if He had no claim on us for the many bigger and smaller sins we have wantonly committed. We are odd penitents, if nothing can persuade us to let even one tiny dish pass at the banquet of life, but insist on every morsel that comes our way.

We profess to be terribly sorry for our sins, but meanwhile we are looking out of the corner of our eye to spy out some chance for a jolly party and rollicking amusement, and we raise Cain if we think we are done out of an hour's enjoyment. Voluntary abandonment of something that pleases our palate or tickles any of our senses never enters our mind.

Is there no danger that our penitence is a piece of make-believe when we seem to have only one anxiety: not to miss anything that is going on? Is it not likely that God expects a little sobriety from sinners? A man who shuns all self-denial offers to God a cheap religion. He may say beautiful prayers when the fancy takes him. He may even sing his hymn and go to church when he feels good and there is nothing else to do. He may talk touchingly about sacred matters and experience genuine emotion when he chances to think about holy things, but the fact remains that it costs him nothing.

The moment there is question of fasting and abstinence, of not going to the movies during Lent, of getting up early on a cold morning to go to Mass, of giving some substantial alms to the poor — an alms that involves a real privation to him — of doing an act of kindness that means some awkwardness and hardship for him, he finds an excuse or boldly says that it is unreasonable to expect such a thing: it would upset his ease or routine or other arrangements and calculations.

Lent makes some people feel uncomfortable. It is good that it should do so. A comfortable religion is not the highest homage to God. Our Lord was not very comfortable while on earth. His true followers must not mind a little voluntary discomfort on the road of life.

﹏

Chapter Thirty-Five

Imitate the repentance of Peter and Paul

Scripture tells that while Peter was lying and cursing that he "knew not the Man," Jesus, turning around, looked at Peter, and Peter remembered and, rushing out, he wept bitterly.[96] Scripture tells that while Paul was on the road to Damascus, breathing threats against the Christians, Christ showed Himself to him, saying, "I am Jesus, whom thou persecutest," and Paul meekly and humbly answered, "Lord, what wilt Thou that I do?"[97] When we acknowledge our sins, we should remember these two fellow sinners, who, forgiven by God's mercy, now reign in glory with Christ.

Thus, we should say, "Lord, look upon us as Thou didst look on Peter! Thou hast shamed us into repentance by one glance of Thy pitying eyes and shown us our ingratitude and our cowardice. We often made big professions of unswerving fidelity, even as Peter did. We said we would go to prison and death with Thee, as Thy boasting apostle did. We said that if others were scandalized in Thee, we would never be. If, by word of mouth, perchance we

---

[96] Matt. 26:74-75.
[97] Cf. Acts 9:5-6.

have not yet under oath denied Thee, our sinful behavior has been such as if we had never known Thee, and onlookers might well have concluded that we did not belong to Thy disciples.

"We forgot Thy warnings, we disbelieved Thy words, we fancied ourselves strong enough to play the hero, we would not watch and pray, lest we should enter into temptation, and, like Peter, we have fallen and played the coward. Look upon me in pity, and bring home to me my shameful weakness and contemptible ingratitude, so that I may hasten away from the occasion of sin and weep bitterly over my fall, even as Peter did and was comforted by Thy appearance to him on Easter Day."

Not all our sins were sins of weakness, like the sin of Peter. On the road of life, we may have been struck down while, in some fierce passion and willful fury, we were on the path of evil. The grace of God pursued us, but we "kicked against the goad"[98] as St. Paul did. We indeed felt the urge, the impulse of our better self under the influence of the Holy Spirit, but we resisted it, struggled and fought against it. We wanted our own way and not God's.

We had a plan and had to carry it out, even against the clamors of our conscience, the protest of our innermost self that we were doing wrong. Anger, pride, or sensuality drove us on to our Damascus with letters of the Devil, the high priest of evil. We tried to confound any man or woman with force or falsehood, if they dared to withstand us. Then God smote us down from our high horse and happily brought us low. Then Jesus appeared to our soul, called us by our name, and said, "Man, why persecutest thou me?" Blessed were we in that His grace overcame us and in that we said, "Lord what wilt Thou have me to do?"

Peter and Paul surely pray for us all, that we, having followed their sin, may follow them in penitence and share with them their glory in Heaven.

[98] Cf. Acts 9:5.

☞

Chapter Thirty-Six

Be deeply sorry for your sins

I am not a saint, and how could I manage to escape Purgatory? Well, there is the famous case of the man, who certainly was not a saint, and who escaped it. Why not imitate him?

And what had he done? Committed murder and robbery. How many times is not precisely on record, but justice finally overtook him. He kept on blaspheming until a couple of hours before his death, and somehow still managed to go straight to Heaven without any Purgatory at all. How do we know that? From the lips of Christ Himself, who said to him on Good Friday afternoon, "This day thou shalt be with me in Paradise."[99]

The man must have stopped blaspheming about one or two o'clock that day, and shortly before sunset, say, about five o'clock, when they had clubbed him to death, breaking his bones, his soul was with his Redeemer in Paradise.

By the grace of God, it evidently can be done. Let us see how he managed it.

He began with the fear of God. The boasting bravado of his mate in the face of death disgusted him. Bad though his crimes had

[99] Luke 23:43.

been, bold and brazen his conduct toward his fellowmen, toward God he would not play the braggart.

The fear of meeting God stole over him. The dread of the majesty and holiness of God overpowered him. He saw his wretched life as it must appear before the righteous anger of infinite sanctity, and he shrank back in terror. People go to Purgatory who lacked a sense of sin, who took God too easily and had little awe for eternal holiness. Mortal sins, once the guilt was absolved in the confessional, ceased to trouble them; and venial sins were in any case only trifles, so they thought. They had never known the fullness of repentance and a humble and broken heart.

The penitent thief, while abhorring his own life, felt a pitying veneration for the Sufferer on the Cross in their midst. Even a criminal can pay homage to innocence and virtue. "This man hath done no evil,"[100] said he, and he resented the mockery of Him by the man crucified on the left. A sinner, he could still love and praise goodness and could feel a reverence for it and even, in a way, a longing for it.

His practice had been deplorable, but he had not lost his ideals. He had sunk in the mire of sin, but he still could look upward and feel there were higher things.

But there are people who perhaps have not fallen as deeply as the penitent thief, but who never had much sense for higher things. They normally kept out of mortal sin, or at least cursorily repented after their mortal sins, for they did not want to be damned. Of higher things, however, they had no idea. They felt no desire, no yearning for them. They always lived and thought on a lower plane. Hence, their sorrow was never very deep, only just enough not to make their confession invalid. As to what they were pleased to call their peccadilloes, they hardly heeded them at all; they never aimed at sanctity or even felt any inclination that way.

[100] Luke 23:41.

It is after such a mean sort of life that such people have to learn in Purgatory that, after all, Heaven is not so cheap and not to be had as a reward for slovenliness. A Mary Magdalene, who has not comfortably settled down to her ways of sin, seems to have more chance of a profound act of contrition, utterly cleansing the soul, than a person who has deliberately taken what we may call "the lower road," without any aspirations for divine heights.

The penitent thief certainly by his very prayer — "Lord, remember me when Thou shalt come into Thy kingdom"[101] — showed that with all his sins, he had not lost the Messianic hope, the sacred dream of every true son of Israel, the promised reign of righteousness in the fullness of time.

He, too, even as Simeon and Anna, had longed for the coming of a Redeemer even in the misery of his sin, and hence, divine grace helped him to see his Savior in the mangled, bleeding, crucified Figure by his side. So, by one mighty act of faith and trust and love, his soul adored and clung to Him whom the crowd of self-righteous Pharisees despised, and that one act, which contained utter penitence and humility, purified his soul and was rewarded by Christ with the promise of Heaven that very day.

> *Happy man,*
> *to escape not only Hell,*
> *but even Purgatory!*
> *A few hours more patience,*
> *bearing your torments on the cross,*
> *a punishment that you loudly but humbly*
> *proclaimed you had merited,*
> *and then rest and joy shall be*
> *yours forever in company with Christ.*
> *May we use our last hours as well as you did,*

[101] Luke 23:42.

and may it not be long between our death
and our entrance into Heaven.

Remember us, O Lord,
Thou who hast already
entered into Thy kingdom,
and delay not our salvation,
although we have been sinners,
and take us to Thyself on the
very day of our death. Amen.

Part Six

Sanctify your home

⌒

Chapter Thirty-Seven

Invite Jesus and Mary
into your marriage

There was a marriage at Cana in Galilee, and Jesus, His Mother, and the Apostles were there. Surely an ideal wedding! Could such a privilege be ever repeated? It is not only repeated, but enhanced, for those Catholics who desire it.

Watch a truly Catholic bridegroom and bride at the nuptial Mass. It is after the Consecration. Christ is present on the altar, as really present as He was at that marriage feast in Cana. Someone who holds apostolic powers, the Catholic priest, stands before the altar. A man and woman enter the sanctuary; they climb the steps of the altar and kneel almost within touch of Jesus and His Apostles. Mary, the mother of Jesus, although not present under sacramental veils, is close by in knowledge and love, for her tenderness knows no distance when there is a feast among the children of God.

The priest gives the kneeling couple a solemn, divine blessing in the name and in the presence of his divine Master, and a few moments later, they partake in Holy Communion of the Sacred Banquet infinitely more marvelous than the wine changed from water at Cana.

Are, then, our newly wedded people less favored than the Galileans in our Lord's day? Was not the feast at Cana a symbol of greater things to come? Yet there are many Catholics who fail to understand it. Although from childhood they may have learned that there are seven sacraments, they somehow seem to think that Matrimony is not really a sacrament like the others. They know, perhaps, that it is not the proper thing not to marry in Church, but they fancy that the civil registrar, for all intents and purposes, is the one who really marries them. The Church, so they think, only adds a special blessing.

But even in the case of better-instructed Catholics, who know that for the baptized, marriage is either a sacrament or it is nothing at all — for sacrament and marriage cannot be separated, and a purely civil contract is no sacrament for a Catholic — even in their case, I say, there is often slovenliness and neglect even though they are married in the Church. So many deliberately, or out of sheer carelessness, are married without the nuptial blessing at Mass.

When they hear their marriage is valid without it, that it is not in itself a mortal sin to do without it, unless it is done out of sheer contempt, when they hear that they will not be eternally damned for it, they smile and say that they will start married life without any solemn divine blessings and joint Communion.

As to Mass and Communion on their wedding day, they are regarded as somewhat superfluous acts of piety they can well do without. They have calculated a dozen times over whom they are going to ask as wedding guests, but Jesus and Mary as wedding guests have never entered their minds. And so they start married life in a mean and paltry way, even though they get a paragraph in the local paper, which describes the bride's dress and gives the names of the guests. Let us hope that bride and bridegroom were at least in the state of grace, for if they lacked that wedding garment, the prettiest gown and the smartest suit are sorry substitutes.

Many a priest has to drive the happy couple into the confessional shortly before the wedding ceremony, lest there should be danger that they should sacrilegiously receive in mortal sin a sacrament of the living. Sometimes even then he does not succeed, and with deepest misgivings he assists at what he suspects is a shameful profanation of a sacrament, however merry may be the tune the organ plays when bride and bridegroom march out.

Can people wonder why marriages entered into in such worldly and slovenly ways, just with the bare minimum to make them valid, so often end in disaster? Married people need so many graces for a peaceful, holy life with one another, for bearing the hardships and responsibilities of home life, for the bringing up of children in the love and fear of God, that a wedding so ungenerous, so ungracious to Almighty God, so unspiritual and mundane, so haphazard and unprepared, so prayerless and without ideals as Catholic weddings sometimes are, must end in disillusion, bitterness, and domestic misery.

A wedding without Jesus and Mary spells ruin, a wedding with these loving guests promises well. Jesus will perform a miracle, if necessary, to make the bride and bridegroom happy, not only in temporal things, or on their wedding day, but in the matters of eternal value, so that, after a life of unselfishness, charity, and forbearance, they may be happy together with their children in God's family above.

Chapter Thirty-Eight

෧

Be charitable toward your family

Christmastime is given to the reunion of the members of families whom the adventures of life have dispersed and often driven far apart. Whatever race or nation may have first chosen this time for such gatherings, the season is well chosen, for it recalls the Incarnation of the Son of God — His entrance into the human family, which has made sacred with a supernatural sanctity every family tie.

There is a homely saying that "blood is thicker than water," and this expresses that even in the natural order, by merely human instinct, the call of the blood is very strong. On the other hand, no fight is so fierce, no hatred so bitter as that between brothers, and family feuds are among the most venomous and lasting. The emotional appeal of reunion at Christmas does a little sometimes and for a little while to soften or suspend the fraternal quarrels, but it is a weak remedy against the disruptive forces of anger or envy or diversity of character.

We need a stronger appeal to conquer the weakness of nature; we need the cry of God incarnate, who Himself became our kith and kin when He did not disdain to be born from a human mother. This cry He uttered to His followers the day before He died: "A new commandment I give unto you, that you love one another. As I have loved you, so you also love one another. By this shall all men know that you are my disciples, if you have love for one another."[102]

And if this passionate cry of our divine Brother, Jesus Christ, is addressed to us, it must surely apply first and foremost to our love for those who are bound to us by the closest ties of nature itself. Surely charity begins at home. Our charity must indeed embrace all men, even our enemies, but who can believe a man who says that he loves even his enemy, but hates his bodily brother, the son of his own mother?

Is there not a tinge of hypocrisy in fostering a feud and maintaining a quarrel with our own brothers or sisters, our own flesh and blood, while overflowing in courtesy and kindness toward those who are comparative strangers to us? Christ told us, "If thou offer thy gift at the altar and there thou remember that thy brother hath anything against thee, leave there thy offering before the altar and go first to be reconciled to thy brother, and then coming thou shalt offer thy gift."[103]

Do we really think that Christ, in here using the word *brother*, used it only in a very general sense to the exclusion almost of those who are really brothers and sisters according to the flesh? There are people who imagine that harsh and bitter words, stinging remarks, hurtful neglect, or ostentatious rudeness are more permissible among the members of a family than toward strangers. As if home were a privileged place for boorishness and anger, and the proper company on which to vent our spleen.

This is an amazing perversion of the natural order and a mockery of Christ's commandment to love one another. Thus families drift apart, and what God has joined together, men break asunder.

[102] Cf. John 13:34-35.
[103] Matt. 5:23-24.

It happens not rarely that a man in early middle age is asked by a friend, "By the way, what happened to your brother whom I met some years ago at your home?" "My brother? Oh, he married and settled down somewhere." "Is he getting on all right?" "I couldn't tell you. I'm not my brother's keeper, am I?" That is what Cain said when Abel's body lay dead on the field.[104]

Now, such a man may not be a physical murderer, but he may be morally so: at least his brother has been dead to him for many a year. He could never stand him when still at home; it was one everlasting quarrel, to the distress of the parents and a darkening of family life. He welcomed the day when he was not obliged to live under the same roof with him. Once parted, he was completely indifferent what happened to him, whether he was alive or dead.

It is idle to prate of the love for humanity and to detest the members of your own household or neglect your next of kin.

It is a not-unknown case of false conscience to slave away at all sorts of charitable works and to overlook the needy. I do not say those next door, but in the very house we live — among those who ought to be our nearest and dearest. May our Brother Jesus Christ teach us the right order of charity and make our homes like unto His home at Nazareth, where divine love reigned, even though the brethren of Jesus according to the flesh, His own nearest kin, in ignorance spoke rudely of Him and repeated the gossip of the crowd.[105]

Thus from our home charity will radiate toward others, and our home will be the center of life and love and example of what Christ wants the human family to be and what He can make it by His grace.

---

[104] Gen. 4:9.
[105] Mark 3:21.

Chapter Thirty-Nine

Make the Faith part
of your family life

"He believed and his whole house":[106] thus ends the Gospel story of the healing of the official's son. It is, indeed, the description of an ideal Catholic family, but it is an ideal that is less often verified nowadays, when mixed marriages have risen to an alarming number. It is, no doubt, true that in the majority of cases, the non-Catholic party faithfully abides by the solemn promises of the Catholic Baptism and education of children. It is even true that sometimes the non-Catholic exceeds the Catholic in steady and virtuous conduct and makes an excellent husband or wife, yet it is a sad pity that more often than not, a Catholic cannot say, "I believe and my whole household."

Although the Catholic party is bound by Church law before marriage to make the solemn promise of never ceasing throughout life in the endeavor of bringing the non-Catholic partner to the Faith, how many Catholics, faintly sincere, no doubt, at the time when they make that promise, take that promise seriously after their wedding day? They are too timorous ever to dare to mention

---

[106] John 4:53.

the subject of religion; it is the one point that is taboo between them. After a while, they get quite accustomed to this absolute reticence; the word *church* must never be mentioned.

Even if the Catholics continue to practice, they have to plough their lonely furrow, each one going his own way, or perhaps there is only one who finds the way to church; the other will lie in bed and read the Sunday newspaper instead of worshiping God. The time comes when, with blind perversity, they almost boast that during the long years of married life, they never once discussed religion. When the children grow up, some continue to practice, and others cease to do so and lapse into indifference, because religion at home was such a half-hearted thing: mother went to church, but father didn't, or vice versa, and all father's or mother's relations were Protestants or went to no church at all.

The Faith seemed to be an unimportant accessory easily dispensed with. Home contained none of the things that endear the Faith to the mind of infancy and entwine it with the heartstrings of childhood. First Communion came and Confirmation and the lovely feasts of the Church's year, but it made no difference in the household, since father and mother did not share the joys of their children. Emblems of the Faith — crucifixes, statues, pictures — were not prominent in the home, for either mother or father was not very keen on them, and of course family prayers there could not be, since father did not know the same prayers as mother — if he knew any. The children's friends were Protestants. Thus, the home was alien to the Faith. Since they soon realized that the great outer world was not Catholic either, the poor children could hardly come to any conclusion other than that religion was just a private affair, which need not influence life very much.

Where the whole household is not Catholic, religion is apt to become chilly and cold. It loses its freedom and spontaneity. It is hampered in the innermost circle of intimacy. It is cribbed, cabined, and confined, and almost forced into a stunted growth.

Make the Faith part of your family life

May God increase the number of families of which the father can imitate the man of the Gospel and say, "I and my whole household believe in the fullness of divine revelation: my wife, my children, and the friends of my choice are Catholics."

Chapter Forty

⌒

Form your children's character

Christians should admire the Holy Family at Nazareth, when God was a child obedient to His immaculate Mother and His holy foster-father, living in a humble home, rich in contentment and sanctity. Still more so, Christian families should imitate the example of home life set by God incarnate and Mary and Joseph, who, with all their poverty, lived a heavenly life within the walls of a workman's cottage in a forgotten village, while "Jesus advanced in wisdom and age and grace with God and men."[107]

Never, probably, in the history of mankind has the sanctity of home life been more threatened than it is today. Social and economic pressures drive mothers into the workplace, and the youngest infant is taken from his mother and father and placed in daycare. Divorce and birth control are like the ominous sickle and hammer that cut and crush all that is holy and good. When marriage is degraded and the parents rebel against God, the respect, the obedience, and the love of the children goes, and home becomes a bit of Hell instead of Heaven. School life for most children from five to fifteen, although it might in itself be necessary

---

[107] Luke 2:52.

and beneficent, can become an encroachment on the dignity and authority of the family. Educational faddists would make it so. Worse still: thousands of parents have begun to think that the education of the child is not really their business at all; the public authorities do that.

Parents think that when they provide wholesome food, warm clothing, and a comfortable bed for their child, they are already model parents, their duties are fulfilled, and nothing else can be expected from them. Let us Catholics be aware of that insidious danger, lest we be contaminated by the spirit of the age. Our home is more than a lodging-house for children, and a mother is more than a landlady providing decent meals at regular hours. The formation of the character of the children is in the parents' hands; schoolteachers are only the parents' delegates. How are we training our children? It is not enough to hug and coddle them sometimes, to give them sweets or pennies.

Here are some sound suggestions. Do not correct your child in front of strangers. Some parents have a most disastrous habit of doing this. As soon as a visitor comes, these parents start reciting their child's peccadilloes. They seem to need outside support, as if their own authority were not enough. It is a serious mistake. You and your child are in a sense one. The child's honor is yours; your honor is his or hers. Do not degrade or humble your own flesh and blood in the presence of outsiders. It is an offense against the family bond. The child resents it and rightly so.

When you correct your child, let it be within the family circle; let it be, if possible, quietly between the child and you alone.

Correct your children in moderation, not all too frequently, and about offenses in which there is some real moral fault. If you thrash them for breaking a plate, what will you do when they break your heart? A child knows full well when he is not really guilty, when he could not help a thing. If, then, he gets punished, he becomes either embittered or just indifferent, and he regards punishment as just a fatality that must be endured. You may pun-ish his negligence or boisterousness, but only if there is some real fault in him and the child ought to have known better.

Never, never let your children play off one parent against the other. No mother should half-secretly grant what the father has refused, or vice versa, or remit a punishment behind the other's back.

Above all, do not quarrel with your children. Rebuke them, punish them if necessary, but do not enter into long, querulous, peevish arguments with them, as if to vent your annoyance.

Never quarrel with your spouse in front of your children. It des-ecrates the home almost more than anything else. It lowers paren-tal dignity; it drags your own position with them through the mud. No king or queen starts a quarrel in public before the eyes of his or her subjects; it would be demeaning themselves. You are the king and queen of your little home, and you should never set aside or profane the sweet royalty God has given you.

Chapter Forty-One

Train your children in virtue

Of St. Anne we know nothing whatever, except that she had a holy husband and a very, very holy daughter. As to her husband, St. Joachim, we may as well apply the simple proverb "Birds of a feather flock together."

Joachim and Anne were God-fearing people; hence, they naturally found one another in holy wedlock. Their marriage had not been a foolish, impetuous whim, caused merely by a pretty face and a handsome bearing. It was not the stupid moonshine affair of film or novel; hence, it was blessed by God with a very holy daughter. Many are the lovely pictures of our Lady as a little girl at the knees of her mother, St. Anne, but the reality must, in a spiritual sense, have been much lovelier still.

True, it was the little girl who was the holier of the two, for at the moment of her conception, when God first created her soul, it was enriched with grace in immaculate purity, but her saintly mother helped her from earliest childhood to increase her treasure, for it was from St. Anne's lips that even Mary first heard of God and the hope of Israel. St. Anne's lips taught her to love God with her whole heart, her whole soul, with all her power and all her strength, for so it was written in the Law of Moses. From St.

Anne's lips, no doubt, Mary first heard of the promise of the Messiah, and how a maiden should conceive and bear a Son and call His name Emmanuel.

Both Anne and Mary knew that the time for the coming of the Redeemer was almost fulfilled — the holy man Simeon and the prophetess Anna in the Temple, knew that — perhaps they spoke of it between themselves, who the favored virgin would be, but neither guessed aright. Since our Lady, after the Annunciation, went to her cousin, St. Elizabeth, and not to her mother, one thinks that St. Anne had then already left this world. On earth, perhaps, St. Anne never knew more than that she had a very, very holy daughter, and thus might die happily, leaving behind her the fruit of a holy marriage.

Blessed, indeed, are those parents whose wedded life is God's instrument in securing a holy childhood. Naturally parents labor to secure for their son a fine career or a rich marriage, but some forget that the finest career for any creature is to have a fine career in the court of God in Heaven; the richest wedding feast is that which the divine King made for His Son, who wishes every human soul for his bride.

Would that parents, from the first moment of their children's birth — nay, before — started to pray, to scheme, to work to place their children well in Heaven by surrounding them with every means of virtue in their earthly home!

Sts. Joachim and Anne,
intercede for Christian fathers and mothers,
so that they may not neglect the supernatural,
eternal, celestial future of their children.

Chapter Forty-Two

Foster in your children a devotion to the Savior

"The children of the Hebrews carrying olive branches, and spreading their garments on the way, went to meet the Lord, crying aloud and saying, 'Hosanna to the Son of David.' "[108] The Gospel tells us that when the chief priests and the scribes heard the children shouting even in the Temple, they were moved with anger and said to our Lord, "Hearest Thou what these say?" And our Lord answered them, "Yea, and have you never read, 'Out of the mouth of babes and sucklings thou hast perfected praise'?"[109]

Hypocrites hate children, and the scribes and the Pharisees were true to type. But sometimes even good and sincere people fail to understand Christ's love for children. It is surely very significant that the Gospel tells of two separate and distinct occasions on which our Lord sternly forbade His disciples who were roughly endeavoring to keep children away from Him, and St. Mark expressly states that our Lord "showed Himself much displeased,"[110]

[108] Cf. Matt. 21:8-9.
[109] Matt. 21:16; Ps. 8:3.
[110] Mark 10:14.

as the Douay translates, or "very indignant," as one might translate, with His own Apostles for their mistaken efforts. Our Lord clinched the matter with the decisive phrase "Theirs is the kingdom of Heaven."

The mistake of the Apostles has been repeated numberless times since then. There are few people who fully grasp the power of children for spiritual things and our fearful responsibility for them.

The souls of children, so fresh from God, so recently raised to supernatural life in Baptism, have an extraordinary aptitude for heavenly things, for the loveliness of Christ and His Mother and His saints. Unless someone is a repulsive brute, he does not need a warning not directly to corrupt children, but many need the warning to be careful not to scandalize them, for to scandalize little ones merits the fierce threat of having a millstone bound around the neck and being cast into the sea.[111] Many more need to be recalled to their duty to foster in children the love of Jesus and of Mary, and of all that those names convey.

It is sometimes argued that children do not understand such things and do not appreciate them, that such things do not impress them.

Some years ago, I stood in the corner of a Catholic cemetery; at first I was quite alone. After a few moments, a little boy of between eight and nine, a fresh-looking, plump little man with light hair, a real Saxon boy, shyly enters, looks quickly around, and thinks that nobody is around. Straight he goes to a grave, at the head of which stands a white marble cross with a figure on it of Christ crucified, almost as big as the small visitor himself. He climbs on the marble edge of the pedestal and throws his arms round Christ's feet. He gives the pierced feet a couple of warm kisses, and then as quickly as his tiny legs can carry him, he runs away. That was in England.

---

[111] Matt. 18:6.

Foster in your children a devotion to the Savior

A dozen schoolchildren come along a country lane; they carry a basketful of marigolds and buttercups that they have woven into garlands. They stop at a monument by the roadside. On a stone base some six feet high and ten feet square there is a great figure of Christ carrying His Cross. He bends forward with one hand supporting Himself on His knee, the other arm around the beam of the Cross. The children clamber up the stone base. They wind their garlands around the Cross — a special little garland to go over the crown of thorns on His head, a special garland over His shoulders. They kiss the stone hands and stroke His face. When the basket is empty, they climb down, kneel for a minute on the grass for a prayer, and then merrily go their way, humming some tune they heard in church. Except the watcher, myself, no adult was anywhere near. That was abroad.

Happy the parents who teach their children to love Jesus crucified; blessed the children who from babyhood have heard that our Lord suffered and died because He loved them and by His Cross wished to redeem the world. Let us remember our Lord's own words: "Unless you become like little children, you shall not enter into the kingdom of Heaven."[112]

[112] Matt. 18:3.

Chapter Forty-Three

☞

Pray for your children

It is to be feared that there are Catholic parents who do not pray for their young children. They somehow seem to think that children are in no need of prayers until they come to the age of reason.

It does not strike such parents that if they prayed for each of their children from the moment they knew that God had created his soul, the child, when coming to the age of discretion, might start conscious life with a treasure stored up for him by many years of the prayers of his father and mother.

There are enough clamoring advertisements calling upon parents to insure their children for the years of their schooling or even their later start in life. Many parents deprive themselves of much, so that their children may begin life with some solid financial advantage, but fewer are the parents who think of securing a spiritual advantage for their children by accumulated riches of prayer in their younger days.

Good parents could almost bind and force the hands of God in favor of their child, for St. Monica[113] is not the only mother to

---

[113] St. Monica (332-387) prayed for more than twenty years for the conversion of her son, St. Augustine (354-430), who

whom God has listened or will listen, lest a child of many tears and prayers should perish.

No doubt parents pray when their child is actually ill, and they beg then for his bodily health. It is good that they should do so, but they should have begun earlier. It would have been wise had they thought of the child's spiritual health as well as of his health of body.

There is such a thing as vicarious prayer and merit. When as yet the child is incapable of praying or meriting, God can infuse additional grace into the child's soul for the sake of others who offer to God their prayers and merits on behalf of the child. Thus, when the first temptations come, the child's soul is strengthened. When the first capacity for prayer and love of God awakens in the child, his power for good is enhanced; his sanctifying grace is at a higher intensity. If the parents had prayed, the child's divine graces would be more numerous; he would leap forward to God, his heavenly Father, more spontaneously and embrace Christ, the Redeemer, more eagerly.

A child whose parents do not pray for him is a half-disinherited child and starts spiritual life in comparative poverty. There are indeed saints canonized who had wicked or negligent parents, but most saints had parents, or at least mothers, who were conspicuous for tender piety, who dedicated their little ones to God. There is no need here to think as far back as St. Monica and St. Augustine. St. John Bosco and St. Thérèse of Lisieux are outstanding examples in more recent times.[114]

If, then, you are in charge of children, parents first, and relatives afterward, pray for the children in your life. Do not wait until

turned from his sinful ways and went on to become Bishop of Hippo.

[114] St. John Bosco (1815-1888), founder of the Salesian Order, and St. Thérèse of Lisieux (1873-1897), Carmelite nun and Doctor, were both known for their childlike spirit.

the news comes that in early manhood or womanhood they have gone astray and succumbed to the allurements of the world. Then you would have to strike your breast and, in bitterness of soul, have to acknowledge that you are partially responsible for the disaster through your neglect. Pray for your children, and you will please the great divine Lover of children, who blessed them when He was on earth and still blesses them from His throne in Heaven.

Part Seven

Love your neighbor

Chapter Forty-Four

Guard your thoughts

From early childhood, we have learned from our catechism that God reads the innermost thoughts of our heart. Our words and deeds, however important, are but the lesser part of our human life; the greater part consists in our inner life, the life of our thoughts.

Our thoughts begin with the first moment of consciousness in the morning and end only with the end of it in sleep. For hours, perchance, we neither speak nor act, but we think. And God reads all our thoughts: our good thoughts and our bad thoughts and our useless thoughts, when we are wool-gathering and dreaming all about nothing and wasting our time.

What a picture they would make if we could film them all and put them on the screen! Dark and ugly scenes when we are sinning in thought, when we covet our neighbor's goods or our neighbor's spouse; black scenes of thoughts of pride, envy, and hatred; repulsive scenes when we think of matters offending modesty and purity.

But then, as we hope, there are also beautiful and noble scenes, when we struggle in prayer, beset with many distractions, and sore distressed with many temptations, but heroically trying to keep our wayward mind steady and fixed on God.

There are grand scenes when we bear our sufferings with inner resignation, out of the love of God; when we make deep acts of faith, hope, love, and contrition; when we forget and forgive injuries done to us and in our hearts pardon our enemies and wish them well; when we are humble and grateful toward God and abandon ourselves completely to His blessed will.

There are blank or gray scenes when idly we let our fancy roam upon airy nothings or half-dangerous imaginings, either wishing for things that can never come to pass or posturing in some self-praise or fancied victory or glorification.

God has seen them all and noted them, for they all count, and count as much for Him as acts and words do. To God, it is the intention that matters. Of this our Lord said so tellingly, "The light of thy body is thy eye. If thy eye be single, thy whole body shall be lightsome, but if thy eye be evil thy whole body shall be darksome. If, then, the light that is in thee be darkness, the darkness itself, how great shall it be!"[115] Yet there are people who mind their thought-life very little; they seem satisfied as long as they have not actually said or done anything wicked.

Their thoughts, they plead, they cannot help. In any case, mere thinking, so they suppose, does not matter much. They are utterly wrong, for thoughts are the source and the root of all good or evil. Thinking precedes speaking or doing, and the whole value of acts and words depends — as far as God and our souls are concerned — on the thought that lies behind them, whereas thoughts have their value independently in themselves.

To keep our thoughts in check is true self-mastery. Even if a person is ever so correct in word or gesture, he may be a demon within, if his thoughts are wrong.

On the other hand, a person's speech and gestures may be clumsy and his outward behavior be blamed or misunderstood, but

[115] Matt. 6:22-23.

if his heart is right, and his thoughts clean, he will be an angel in God's sight, no matter how much his fellowmen may scorn him. God is the searcher of heart and reins, and He saves the upright of heart, says the Scripture.[116] St. Paul wrote to the first Christians, "The peace of God, which surpasseth all understanding, keep your hearts and minds in Christ Jesus. Whatsoever things are true, whatsoever modest, whatsoever just, whatsoever holy, whatsoever lovely, whatsoever of good fame, if there be any virtue, if anything praiseworthy, think on these things."[117]

Indeed, think on such like things and not on things that pollute the heart and stain the mind, forever, perhaps, unknown and undiscovered by men, but always plainly known to God.

[116] Cf. Ps. 7:10-11 (RSV = Ps. 7:9-10).
[117] Phil. 4:7-8.

Chapter Forty-Five

Control your speech

Restraint in speech is one of the most difficult virtues to practice. There is no harm whatsoever in finding through speech both amusement and relaxation, no harm, in fact, in talking for the sake of talking, for the need to talk is a very real one in human nature.

Man is made to exchange thoughts with his fellows. Let two friends sit in the corner of the hearth and continue their confidential chatter to their hearts' content; it is but innocent recreation; it is but a proof of their mutual friendship. The conversation of saints is like a melody to God, but it is such a pity that speech is so much abused through vanity, unkindness, and impurity.

Through vanity some people can talk only of themselves, and their talk is overt or hidden self-praise. They know no other topic than the excellency of their own sayings and doings. They want only to talk so that others may know how clever, how good, and how virtuous they are. Every sentence is uttered to feed their pride. Some annoy their audience by clumsy boasting, but many are much shrewder, and, with judicious art, only now and then insert a cunning phrase to impress the hearer with their superior intelligence, capacity, and nobility of soul.

They bring the conversation around so that they may shine, and if they do not succeed in showing to advantage, they think the time of conversation is lost. They must, of course, pretend interest in what their companion says, but it is only feigned; they wish him to finish quickly, so that they may return to their favored theme: the wonders of their own shrewdness, goodness, and talent.

Thus, their conversation lacks all affection and tenderness, all wish to please, to soothe, to charm, all desire to quicken wit with news and knowledge. It is not an interchange of good things, a give-and-take of the mind's treasures and gifts of imagination. It becomes just selfish parading and vulgar vanity. More, it is mean and sinful.

The sin may not be mortal, but it is sin nonetheless — this self-worship, this singing of hymns to our own divinity, forgetful that we owe all to God except our sins, which are our own.

There is, however, another and greater abuse of speech: the unwarranted discussion and revelation of our neighbors' faults. Blessed is the man who does not thus sin by his tongue. Malignant gossip is the blight and the curse of much conversation. Some indulge in it with lesser malice, for lack of other matter, and because they know that dissecting their neighbor's character usually finds eager listeners.

A little bit of scandal will greedily be swallowed as a spicy morsel. It will set people talking with zest, however languid the conversation may have been before. "We meant no harm," they sometimes say, "but we must talk about something." Harming another man's reputation becomes just a pastime, and a disgraceful pastime it is! Others, however, do it with malice aforethought. They take an angry, envious pleasure in running other people down.

Such talkers betray an embittered, disappointed, hateful disposition; they love to vent their spleen in tales of other people's iniquities. They have a grievance against mankind and, with spiteful glee, revel in the faults, sins, failings, and miseries of all and sundry. If a person is reputed virtuous, good, and saintly, they will just show that person up and let it be known what that person is really made of — just our common clay, and dirty clay at that. The speech of such talkers is just venom, spat from a mouth hissing with hate, contempt, gloating over evil, desire to degrade, to drag down what might dwarf their own despicable self.

There is a third abuse of speech that is distressfully common. It goes by the name of telling lurid stories, innuendoes, jokes with double meanings, and witticisms in which the wit consists only in the suggestion of the indecent.

St. Paul tells us that there are things that should not even be named among the saints,[118] but these foul talkers have no such scruple. Nothing is sacred to them, if they think they can raise a snigger or a dubious laugh by their remarks. It is a disgusting habit.

Yet many factories, clubs, offices, and parlors reek with it. It is supposed to be fun, but it is fit only for the gutter. What the lowest comedian would not dare to say to his public, however little squeamish it might be, sometimes passes from mouth to mouth with a smirk and a grin among reputedly respectable people. The more this vice is indulged in, the less its vicious and loathsome character is realized, and people who indulge in it sink ever deeper in the mire.

The tongue that God gave to man to sing God's praises, and to help other men to Heaven, is prostituted to beastliness. If anyone should feel even a slight rebuke of conscience for not being quite free of this practice, let him dedicate his tongue again to God and cleanse it from the defilement of this world.

[118] Eph. 5:3.

⌒

Chapter Forty-Six

Avoid judging others

"Judge not before the time, until the Lord come."[119] This puts us in mind of His Second Coming, on the clouds of Heaven, to judge all mankind. Many of us are given to rash judgment and recklessly anticipate the great day, as if we were endowed with infinite wisdom and could read men's hearts and measure the course of all human history.

Scripture bids us to be slow in judging, for we know very little. Judging does not here refer to clear and timely decision in points of our duty and conduct, as if we had to be halting and hesitating whenever we are called upon to decide what to do. It refers to those swift, unreasoned, impulsive opinions we often form of our neighbor's conscience, his aims and intentions, as if the secrets of his heart were an open book to us.

It refers to those cruel condemnations of other people when we have not the wherewithal upon which to base our opinion. It refers to those sinister suggestions of other people's motives and ideas, those evil interpretations of words and actions, for which we either have no grounds whatsoever, or at most flimsy reasons,

---

[119] 1 Cor. 4:5.

insufficient to move any unbiased person, reasons that we would scorn if other people used them to argue about us.

We sometimes speak about others or act toward them as if the Last Day were already over and gone, as if we had been present and heard the Judge give sentence: "Get away from me, ye cursed, into everlasting fire!"[120] And when we examine our own conscience, we have to acknowledge that our ideas were prompted by some paltry prejudice rather than by sound reason. We put on the black cap and condemn some unfortunate creature to moral death before bothering to sift any evidence.

We did it because we happened to be in a bad mood; we did it out of foolish exuberance of animal spirits, as if it were sport to give a death blow to a man's character. We did it because we are suspicious by nature; we are victims of that dismal disease of seeing evil everywhere, as a drunkard sees snakes.

Our Lord promised the Apostles that, at the Judgment, they would sit on twelve thrones to judge the twelve tribes of Israel.[121] We are no apostles, we have not waited until Judgment Day, but we are continually on some self-erected throne, judging all and sundry with great display and pomp of omniscience.

"I can tell you why he did this!" "I know him through and through!" "I can see through the thin veneer of his piety!" "I understand his dark designs!" "That man is full of ambition, uncleanness, and dishonesty — be warned by me!" Such are our pontifical pronouncements, without any guarantee of infallibility, thrown out at random with a schoolboy's rashness.

The good name and fame of scores of people lie in wrack and ruin about us; we have roused hatred and envy, broken friendships, started feuds and quarrels, but unheeding we go our way, quite pleased with our superior insight and rectitude. Thank God not

[120] Cf. Matt. 25:41.
[121] Matt. 19:28.

many go thus far: they sin by rash judgment only in thought; they happily keep their thoughts to themselves. In such cases, their sin is indeed less, yet it remains a sin after all.

Even in the secrecy of our heart, we may not needlessly sit in judgment on the lives of others. Sometimes, indeed, we must regulate our own conduct on our honest, well-considered trust or distrust of others, but often and again we are tempted to do so without any justification at all: a mere fruitless, uncalled-for speculation, a groundless thinking of evil without justification and necessity.

God, who reads our thoughts, will call us to account for the pride, the envy, and the heartlessness that underlie our rash, tacit condemnation of our neighbor. Let us remember the proverb "A man judges others by himself." A good man does not lightly think evil of his brother; a bad man thinks others as bad as himself.

By imputing motives, a man betrays his own soul; he reveals the motives that are the usual reasons for his own actions. A saint is the last person to think another a sinner and the first to find an excuse, or a mitigating circumstance, or even a laudable explanation on noticing something that at first looks like an evil deed.

Let us banish from our souls any dark, uncharitable thoughts and force ourselves to think well of others whenever possible. If, on examining our conscience, we find that we have harbored unfounded suspicions, let us drive them away for Jesus' sake. He has shown us mercy beyond our deserts; let our thoughts be merciful, even as His are. Thus embracing all the world in charity, we shall in true happiness live in preparation for Christ's Second Coming, when He shall come to us as a Savior as well as a Judge.

Chapter Forty-Seven

‿

Avoid speaking ill of others

"Be swift to hear, but slow to speak": this is the admirable advice St. James gives us.[122] How great is the evil done by hasty speech, and how often do we ourselves recognize this when it is too late! We bite our lips in bitter regret and mutter to ourselves, "I wish I had never spoken." Our neighbors may have ten times grumbled and groaned, "If only that person had kept silent, what mischief would have been prevented. But some people must talk!" Let us see what causes lead to disastrous abuse of the tongue.

They seem to be threefold: first, the desire to be interesting; second, motives of secret envy; and third, sudden explosions of anger.

So we know a spicy bit of news and are burning to tell others. To feel really important for a moment and to be the center of eager curiosity, to have wondering, questioning eyes fixed upon us and ears drinking in every syllable we say: that is the real reason we cannot keep this wretched scrap of scandal to ourselves. By breaking silence, we tear our neighbor's character to shreds; we may shatter friendships, destroy the peace of homes, perchance ruin a

---

[122] James 1:19.

man's or a woman's career, but somehow we must tell. We are bursting with it. Why? For a moment's silly gratification.

Perhaps we were told in confidence, or got to know by sheer chance and had no right to know. Every instinct of honor and virtue suggested that we should keep our knowledge to ourselves. Our unfortunate victim, even though at fault, has a right to his or her good name and fame and begged us not to speak, yet we must talk and have our delicious five minutes when our foolish lips are watched for every savory sound of sad and sorry secrets. When we have finished, we are inwardly ashamed of what we have done and would blush if it were found out that we had spoken.

Of course, we adjure our listeners not to tell a soul, but mostly in vain, for they follow our example and must tell. We have wrought evil, perhaps great evil, and what for? Our cruel tongue has metaphorically murdered a fellowman for less than a farthing, for the sickly sweet of a moment's mental vanity: that we knew what the others did not.

But frequently an even darker and more malignant motive makes us open our mouth. It is envy. We find a nasty pleasure in degrading others and lowering the esteem in which they are held. This envy is often secret; in fact, we may be only half-conscious of it ourselves, but it is real nonetheless. We dislike people being made too much of; it seems to lessen our own position, for we feel ourselves at least as good as they. We intend to take down that reputed saint a peg or two. We know something about him or her that will surprise people. It will show that saint in true colors and prove true the proverb that even giants have feet of common clay. Hence, although we mask our real reason with many protestations of sorrowful surprise, we find a sort of malicious joy in telling what we know against him.

We assure our listener that only duty made us speak; we beg our listener not to think less of the party in question because of what we felt bound to tell. But all this may be only a flimsy sham. Our guardian angel reads our conscience better. It is a mixture of hypocrisy with envy, and if in an honest mood we examine ourselves, we cannot deny it.

A third kind of abuse of the tongue is the outcome of anger, and St. James had this no doubt mainly in view. What strange, unnatural, preposterous things are said in an outburst of passion!

A few minutes afterward, we assure our victim that we did not really mean the things we said; we try to explain them away; we beseech him to forget them, blot them totally out of his memory, and so forth. But the mischief is done. It may take years, perhaps a lifetime, to undo the effects, or again, they may never be undone this side of the grave. What we said with remorseless, ruthless swiftness we have to repent of at leisure. Good for us if our opponent does not answer, since he knows and pities our tantrums, but if he answers, a battle royal has begun, and as the quick words follow, they increase in brutality or in venomous power to hurt. Hatred and fury is the result, and the world is filled with misery that has its origin in the thoughtless, uncontrolled misuse of the tongue.

May prudence and prayer act as bridles to that small but unruly member. "Think before you speak," we often say to our children; we ought to say it often to ourselves, for adults suffer as much from this danger as do the young ones. When the peril is upon us, let us sign our mouth with the Sign of the Cross and pray: "Do Thou, Lord, open my lips, and my mouth shall utter Thy praise."[123] Praise, and not scandal or invective of others — praise of God forever and ever.

---

[123] Cf. Ps. 50:17 (RSV = Ps. 51:15).

Chapter Forty-Eight

⤳

Avoid boasting and seeking praise

The second letter to the Corinthians gives details of St. Paul's life that otherwise we might never have known. It is clear that the task of speaking about himself at this length was utterly distasteful to the apostle. It seemed to make him almost ashamed of himself, and a verse or so further on in the chapter he actually says, "I am become foolish; you have compelled me."[124]

So it is with saintly people. They hate referring to themselves for the purpose of receiving praise and admiration. It is not so with the common run of us. We love a bit of praise or high esteem. It is honey to us and a delicious delicacy. Even if our neighbor lays on flattery thick, as with a trowel, we enjoy it and can never have enough of it. There is a process known as angling with sly solicitations for praise, and we indulge in it with childish persistency. There are people who unblushingly lengthen a conversation, which only consists of "I, I, I, and always I."

Others are shrewder, but not less egotistic. They know that it is against good manners to mention oneself too frequently; hence, they await their opportunity, when with feigned unconcern they

[124] 2 Cor. 12:11.

can slip in a few remarks that redound to their honor. They may even protest that the last thing in the world they desire is praise for what they have done, although in their heart of hearts, it is precisely their longing for self-aggrandizement that prompted their seemingly casual reference to themselves.

It is an old saying: "Out of the abundance of the heart the mouth speaks."[125] It is indeed their secret, overweening self-importance that brings their words to their lips, whereas it is the Christian Faith that makes us think little of ourselves and makes us avoid any occasions for self-display. Such self-display should be shunned, not only because it is a breach of socially correct conduct, not only because it is repulsive to others or makes us ridiculous in their eyes, but because it is unseemly in a disciple of our Lord Jesus Christ.

Are we vain of some natural gift that we fancy we possess? Even supposing that we possess it, have we bestowed this gift upon ourselves? Are we our own creators? Are we vain about some gift that we have acquired by study, practice, and perseverance? Let us say to ourselves, "If others had my opportunities, would they not have done as well as I, or even better? Have they perhaps not gifts in another direction as great as mine, however much they may differ from mine? I am a splendid cook, but I have no head for management, or perhaps I am a first-class manager, but I am no great scholar, or perhaps I am a great scholar, but I cannot sing or dance or play or paint."

Thus, with a little common sense and goodwill, I will soon come to the conclusion that I am not the only pebble on the beach and that my imagined superiority does not come to much, and that it is rather an unworthy performance to play the peacock about it so very often.

How much grander, how much nobler for a man to see, to acknowledge, to admire, and to praise the gifts of others than, with

[125] Matt. 12:34.

sickly self-complacency, to contemplate his own! From such morbid contemplation springs jealousy, meanness, envy, and hatred. How much more truly Christian it is to look away from ourselves and to look up to the infinite goodness and perfection of God!

When we gaze upon the majesty and beauty of our Lord, we begin to shrink in our own estimation and to feel ourselves the poor, paltry, unsatisfactory, frail creatures we are. We may think ourselves big fellows in comparison with our next-door neighbor, but we are but dwarfish imps when we look down upon ourselves from the height of God's mountains. The angels must think us half-witted creatures when they see us strut about here on earth, all trying to look half an inch taller than the man next to us, all crowing about our own doings and achievements as if they were the last word in the universe.

We sometimes have a good laugh at the absurd boasting of advertisements, but, if we examine our consciences, we are bound to ask ourselves whether we look less absurd in the sight of Heaven with our strange boastings of our own personal perfections and personal achievements.

"All alone have I done it," we seem to say in laughable pride and childish ostentation, instead of acknowledging, "By the grace of God, I am what I am, and I hope that the grace of God has not been in vain in me."[126] Thus, we Christians must be modest in self-praise, modest in our wish for the praise of others, and leave to the pagan, godless world all bragging and boasting.

When we have refrained from lauding ourselves to the sky, God may say to us one day, "Well done, thou good and faithful servant. Because thou hast been faithful in little things, I shall set thee over great ones. Enter into the kingdom of Heaven."[127]

[126] Cf. 1 Cor. 15:10.
[127] Cf. Matt. 25:21.

☞

Chapter Forty-Nine

Forgive others

St. Paul repeats what his divine Master had said: that our whole duty toward our fellowmen can be summed up in the command-ment "Love thy neighbor as thyself."[128] But there is this difficulty: our neighbor can be so unlovable, so repulsive, so aggressive, so mean, so degraded, so hateful that we say to ourselves that the impossible is here commanded. We simply cannot conquer our aversion, our loathing and detestation. We cannot help hating the very sight of him!

It is the fashion in certain circles to make in such cases an appeal to "our common humanity" to instill in us pity and pardon toward our weak and erring fellowman, however unattractive he may be. The appeal is, of course, valid as far as it goes, but it does not go very far. On the mere natural plane, there is no motive strong enough to make us conquer the natural shrinking, the natural contempt, and the natural hatred for what seems to us ugly and hostile.

Humanitarianism may fill us with tender emotions when the weather is fair, but it is powerless to overcome the storms of fierce

---

[128] Cf. Rom. 13:8, 10.

antagonism that sometimes rage in human hearts. We need a stronger, supernatural motive. How dare I hate my neighbor, for whom Christ died as He died for me?

There is the story of the fully armed knight who meets his deadly enemy unarmed and helpless on a lonely road. Out flashes his sword; he is ready to strike. His enemy stretches out his arms in the form of a cross and murmurs, "It is Good Friday! Have mercy, for the sake of Christ crucified!" The sword goes back into the scabbard. The knight leaps from horseback and embraces his foe, saying, "Let us be friends, for Christ died for both of us."

It is best to acknowledge that sometimes it requires an almost superhuman effort to overcome our aversion and our resentment when we are thwarted or injured unjustly. If only we would at the same time acknowledge that there is One who can give us grace for this act of self-conquest: Jesus Christ, our Lord, who taught us to pray, "Forgive us our trespasses as we forgive those who trespass against us." Those who are engaged in the fierce struggle of trying to conquer their vehement dislikes, their bitter feelings against someone, should take refuge in the arms of Christ and, in that embrace, draw strength from His Sacred Heart to control their passionate anger and to forgive as they themselves hope to be forgiven.

It would surely be a monstrous thing to receive our blessed Lord in Holy Communion, clasp Him to our bosom, whisper words of worship and endearment to Him, and at the same time breathe fire and slaughter against some fellowman whom we cannot abide. Will our Lord accept our homage if we say to Him, "I love You, but I hate this brother or sister of mine"? Does it not stand written that he who says that he loves God but hates his neighbor is a liar?[129] Has not our Lord Himself told us, first to be reconciled to our brother and then to come and offer our gifts at His altar?[130]

[129] 1 John 4:20.
[130] Matt. 5:23-24.

Such thoughts help a man while he is fighting down his wrathful passions and trying to calm his wild and stormy cravings for revenge. No doubt his lower, merely natural self will argue against his higher self, "But my enemy is a vile character. He is plastered over with sin. He is God's enemy as well as mine!" Christ will answer, "Even if he is now in sin, does that make it certain that he will die in sin? If he dies repentant, will you not share your eternity with him? Even if he is now in sin, have you never sinned and been forgiven? He has offended you, but have you never offended anyone else?"

You may retort, "He has offended me wantonly; he has no excuse." To which Christ would answer, "No excuse? Are you such a searcher of hearts, such a knower of consciences? Can you probe a man's mind so deeply as to be certain there was no excusing circumstance whatever? On Calvary I found an excuse for those who drove the nails into my hands and feet, and pleaded, 'Father, forgive them, for they know not what they do.' The person who offended you has surely not crucified you yet!"

Thus Christ persuades those who truly come to Him not to break the law of charity or to exclude anyone from the bond of love. But from Christ comes more than just outward persuasion by grace to do what is more than human, to do what is heroic, to love your enemies, to tear up the roots of hatred. Blessed are those who, in that bitter battle for self-mastery, beg for help from above, for their prayer will be heard, and in the strength that comes from supernatural aid, they will be able to continue to say with truth, "Forgive us our trespasses as we forgive those who trespass against us. Amen."

⌒

Chapter Fifty

Be willing to work with others

A young lad is awakened by some suspicious and stealthy tramping outside in the narrow streets of Jerusalem. He throws a cloak over his night-gear and is at the door, peeping into the dark. They are dragging Jesus of Nazareth to the house of Annas, the high priest. The lad knows how his widowed mother worships the Prophet from Galilee; hence, he creeps along behind the crowd to see what is going to happen. Soon he is noticed, and one of the mob makes a grab at him, but the night favors the youth. He wriggles out of the man's grasp, but has to leave his cloak in the man's hands.

The youth is St. Mark, and his house is a meeting-place for the followers of Jesus. Thus did the second Evangelist, as a boy, come in touch with the Savior of the world. The Passion, death, and Resurrection of Christ, the Ascension and the marvels of Pentecost are burned into the soul of his boyhood. When, not many years later, his uncle, St. Barnabas, starts with St. Paul on his missionary journeys to preach Christ, the nephew goes with him. After helping the apostles in Cyprus, he goes back to Jerusalem, but soon again he is with his uncle, preaching the gospel.

St. Barnabas clings to St. Peter, and St. Mark becomes St. Peter's assistant. St. Peter affectionately calls him his "son" and sends his greetings to the Christians in Asia Minor. St. Mark travels much and founds the Church in Alexandria in the name of St. Peter. Later he is in Ephesus again, and St. Paul begs St. Timothy to bring him with him to Rome, "for he is so useful to me in the ministry."[131]

St. Mark had carefully taken down in writing the stories St. Peter used to tell in his sermons about the wonders of our Lord's life. He made a book of it and showed it to Sts. Peter and Paul; they fully approved and made him spread it among the faithful as the Gospel, as St. Peter used to tell it. The Church accepted it as inspired by the Holy Spirit and acknowledged him as the second of the Four Evangelists. St. Mark, then, stands out as a willing helper, not so much a leader as an assistant, content to be a second in command to Sts. Peter and Paul, Sts. Barnabas and Timothy, happy to give his services to others and combine with them in furthering the cause of God.

It is a rare gift to be able to work with others. So many people say with angry contempt, "I will not play second fiddle to anyone!" "I will not be somebody's doormat!" "I will do things my own way or not do them at all." It is a pity that so many a noble cause is wrecked because good people will not be content with just being useful, as St. Mark was to the Apostles. No, they must be in command, they must lead, they must be first, or they retire sulkily and refuse to do anything at all.

In secular affairs, when it is a question of their bread and butter, people do not mind it so much. They take it as inevitable. No business can be run with everybody as principal and no one as servant. Hence, people settle down to being employees and submitting to a head, chief, or boss, as they call him. But in voluntary work, and especially in work for God and the Church, this sad frailty often works havoc. Many promising undertakings come to

---

[131] Cf. 2 Tim. 4:11.

nought because the promoters have quarreled. They were zealous indeed, but their zeal did not fit in with the zealous plans of others. Rather than yield, they let the whole thing go to ruin.

Sometimes, of course, it is sheer pride, a wish to lord it over others, the craving to command. Under much pretense of humility, there lurks a haughty soul. Sometimes it is just vanity, sometimes childish vanity, indeed, a pitiful wish for some recognition, an inferiority complex, which imagines slights where none are intended.

We cannot all be chairmen, presidents, or vice presidents; somebody must do the work, the drudgery, if you like, while the other people's names appear in print. Sometimes it is neither pride nor vanity, but the very impetuosity of blind zeal, a narrowness of mind, an obstinacy of will that can make good people so difficult, so angular, so hard to use in combination with others. They have one-track minds; outside the line of their thought, they can see nothing, and within that line, they rush forward without restraint or prudence. They scorn counsel and help; they must do everything themselves. They are completely sure of success, and when, instead of success, failure comes, they are either in despair and throw everything over or, undaunted, they try another individual scheme with the same headlong, precipitate zeal.

May God give us that unselfishness, humility, and simplicity of heart, that mellowness of mind whereby we are able to work with others, even perhaps in a subordinate capacity, and so further on earth the glory of God in company with many brethren.

Chapter Fifty-One

⁀

Lead others to Christ

What draws converts to the Catholic Faith? A few are converted by abstract reasoning. Some read themselves into the Catholic Church. Some are attracted by the beauty of her worship. But the vast majority come into contact with someone to whom his religion was a forceful reality, and they catch the blessed contagion from him.

Of whom of us can it be said, "So-and-so is a Catholic because he met you"? Let us examine our conscience and ask ourselves, "Is there anyone who, by the grace of God, became a Catholic because he met me?" Let there be no false humility. All indeed is due to God's grace, but God does use human means. We may be those human means. If we have never been the means of a conversion, why is that?

There is a text that says, "Let your light shine before men."[132] If we have not shone before men, what is the reason? Well, I cannot pose as a model Catholic, says someone. Friend, no one asks you to pose. A burning candle on a candlestick does not pose as a light; it *is* a light. If the Faith really burns within us, if we are

---

[132] Matt. 5:16.

consumed with fervor for God's truth and God's grace, we are of necessity a light to all and sundry for miles around. Let us shine as Christ wants us to shine, since He called us the children of the light. Nothing shines more attractively than charity. "Hereby shall the world know that you are my disciples, that you love one another."[133]

If, in this scratching, biting, snarling crowd of worldlings, there is a man who is considerate, kind, and meek, may they say, "That must be a Roman Catholic." If, in this cold, calculating, commercial system, where all say, while they trample on their neighbor, "Trade is trade, and you cannot run a business on sentiment," there is a person who shows that there are higher things than financial success, may they say, "That surely is a Roman Catholic."

If, on the other hand, they come to the conclusion from our behavior that Catholics are as hard, as unfeeling, as selfish, as avaricious, and as unforgiving as the rest, our light has become darkness, and they will not be brought to Christ through us.

Of all the possible means of conversion, charity is beyond all doubt the strongest. In fact, in most cases, it is the only means of access to the human heart, and through the heart to the head. If Catholics were model fellow workers, and model neighbors, they would be the most persuasive convert-makers imaginable. They would be mighty apostles. Their practical eloquence would be irresistible.

If only we could show others that Catholicism is kind — show them not by theory and logic, but by the supreme practical argument of Catholic conduct — the masses would flock to the truth of Christ.

None of us should say, "I have no influence with the masses. What I do is of no importance whatever." We would be wrong in our self-depreciation. Our circle may be small, but experience tells

___

[133] John 13:34.

us that the whole world is small. Our personal conduct is like a pebble thrown into a pool. The first ripples make small circles, but they become wider and wider until they reach the outermost edge.

The biggest movements have started from apparently insignificant beginnings. The most colossal statue is copied from a tiny model. We should not say to ourselves, "Nobody takes notice of me. Besides, they do not know that I am a Catholic." We only flatter ourselves that our conduct is unobserved or not commented on. People are silent in our presence; perhaps that is good politics, but wait until our back is turned, and we are under discussion with amazing frankness.

We discuss our employers and fellow employees often enough, and it is only moonshine to imagine that others do not discuss us. They do not know that you are a Catholic? That is a pity! That is a shame! Has nothing betrayed you? Have you kept your religion, your deepest conviction, the very life of your soul so secret that no one could guess it? Then, indeed, you have not been a shining light and have drawn no one to Christ, the Light of the World. If that is so, it is the time to change, for such deliberate secrecy is close to denial, and it stands written, "If anyone deny me before men, I shall deny him before my Father, who is in Heaven."[134]

We should see to it that the secret leaks out that we are Catholics, the favored children of God.

[134] Cf. Matt. 10:33.

Chapter Fifty-Two

Pray for the conversion of unbelievers

Leaving the district of Tyre, Jesus went by Sidon to the lake of Galilee, going right through the Ten Town country, the Gospel tells us.[135] Christ then left Palestine and made a long circuit through pagan land. The Gospels tell us three very striking things of our Lord's transit through this heathen territory.

First is the story of the Phoenician woman, who asked for the cure of her daughter. Pagan as she was, she realized that she had no right to the dainties of God's table, but, after all, she said, "little dogs are allowed to eat under the table of the crumbs of the children." Whereupon our Lord answered, "O woman, great is thy faith; be it done unto thee as thou wilt," and her daughter was cured from that hour.[136]

Then there is the terrible and mysterious scene of the raving maniac possessed by the devils, the man who lived like a naked beast in some disused caves near Gadara and terrorized the neighborhood. When Jesus passed, the man leapt out of the tomb in which he was hidden and shouted, "What have I to do with thee,

---

[135] Mark 7:31.
[136] Mark 7:25-30.

Jesus, Son of the Most High God? Torment me not!" Our Lord said, "Go out of him, thou unclean spirit!" And the devils, whose name was Legion, for they were many, begged to be allowed to go into a herd of swine feeding close by. Christ gave leave, and forthwith the vast herd of about two thousand hurled itself into the lake. The man returned to calmness and sanity. Clothed and in his right mind, he wanted to follow our Lord as His disciple, but Jesus told him, "Go into thy house to thy friends, and tell them how the Lord had mercy on thee." The man went his way and published in all the Ten Towns the great things Jesus had done to him.[137]

Clearly the fame of Christ's deeds had swiftly spread, for a great crowd of people brought Him a man deaf and dumb and besought Christ to cure him. Christ took him apart and gave him speech and hearing. There must have been some great ill in the man, for the Gospel tells us Christ uttered a moan while He cured him. And the moan of the Son of God while He looked up to Heaven surely indicates some great evil, which only divine power could remove.[138]

In these three miracles wrought in pagan surroundings we may well see a symbol of the state of the heathen world: the possibility of great faith, as in the Canaanite woman; the terrible power of the devils enslaving men, as they had enslaved the Gadarene maniac; and great personal misery and helplessness, as in the deaf and dumb man.

The pagan world lies in evil, for the Devil still reigns there, as the missionaries testify. He reigns because the sacrament of Baptism has not yet restricted his realm. Even in Christian countries, when Baptism is neglected, the dark power of devilry begins to raise its head again. Demonic possession is not a thing just to be laughed out of court. There are many devils who roam about the

[137] Mark 5:1-20.
[138] Mark 7:32-35.

world for the ruin of souls. The bodies of swine are indeed their proper dwelling, but where men are unbaptized and unanointed and without sanctifying grace, sin may open the door even for the possession of the bodies of men.

In Christian lands, where men can listen to God's revelation and understand, where men can speak to God in prayer, although there may be many a fall, there is hope of rising after stumbling, of mending after illness. But where men are deaf and dumb, deaf to God's voice and dumb so as never to pray to the God who made them, there, indeed, the depth of misery is great, so great that it would bring a groan of pity to the lips of God incarnate and need, as it were, the blessed fingers of Christ in their ears and on their tongue to make them listen and speak. Yet the grace of God is greater than any human wretchedness, and where there is humility, there is a door open for faith.

The pagan centurion who begged for healing for his servant and said, "O Lord, I am not worthy that Thou shouldst enter under my roof," heard Christ's praise: "I have not found such great faith in Israel."[139] The Canaanite woman who wanted only the crumbs that fall from the master's table and are eaten by dogs heard Christ's wonder at her words and His cry "O woman, great is thy faith."

Let us pray today for the heathen world, so much more numerous than the world that today believes in Christ. Let us pray, for it is we who are to blame that they are heathen still. Our hatreds, our envy, our lukewarmness, and our evil example have retarded the conversion of mankind. Let us pray that Christ may cure their miseries and open their ears and their lips, that Christ may drive out the legions of demons that dwell in their hearts, and that they may have not merely the crumbs from God's table, but the plenty of the eternal banquet, being with us the children of God.

[139] Matt. 8:8, 10.

Part Eight

Grow holier
through the sacraments

Chapter Fifty-Three

☞

Participate in the Mass

St. Peter tells us to have a ready answer for everyone who asks us a question about our religion.[140] Suppose, on our way to Sunday Mass, we were asked, "Where are you going?" What would be the best answer? The best answer would be "To Calvary!" No doubt our questioner would be surprised, as he would not know a place in the neighborhood called by that name; hence, we should explain: "To Calvary, for I am going to Mass." His eyes would probably still show amazement and question us; we should therefore explain further.

The Mass is the continuation of Calvary; it is, in fact, the perpetual sacrifice of Christ by which His Redemption is applied to mankind. If our puzzled friend stammered out, "Christ's torments, agony, and death: are they still going on?" our answer would be easy. "No. Christ, having died once, dies now no more, as the Scripture says,[141] but the act by which Christ offered His sacred humanity to His Father as a victim for sin, allowing it to be sundered and dissolved in death, is not over and done. Holy Writ

---

[140] 1 Pet. 3:15.
[141] Cf. Rom. 6:9-10.

twice tells us that Christ is ever living, making intercession for us.[142] He is the High Priest, who has entered the Holy of Holies, but He is acting as High Priest still. He does not show His wounds to His Father in idle remembrance."

Christ has instituted the mystery of the Mass, so that He, together with us and through our hands, might make the offering still: the oblation of His very self, His Flesh and His Blood, His soul and His body, unto forgiveness of sins. He was the Victim of atonement, not merely for three hours on Golgotha. He is the Lamb of God still who takes away the sins of the world.[143]

On the Cross, it was He alone in person who made the Sacrifice, but now He has joined His brethren with Himself to make the oblation, which is ever pleasing, ever pleading in the sight of God. We now show forth the death of Christ, until He comes, as Holy Scripture says.[144] He remains indeed in glory on His throne in Heaven, and yet, by a miracle of His condescending bounty, He lays Himself, shorn of outward glory, on our altars under the humble appearances of bread and wine.

These appearances, separate as they are, the one a sign of His Body, the other a sign of His Blood, sacramentally signify His death, when His bloodless body *did* hang upon the Cross and all His Precious Blood was spilled upon the ground. Thus, in sign and token only does He die, but in very deed and awesome reality is the oblation of the divine Victim continued by Him in union with us. He places His sacred self into our hands, so that we might offer Him as He offers Himself. Thus the Blood of the New Covenant is ever speaking and crying for mercy from our altars louder than the blood of innocent Abel ever cried for vengeance from the earth.

[142] Rom. 8:34; Heb. 7:25.
[143] Cf. John 1:29.
[144] 1 Cor. 11:26.

Such is the sacrifice of the Mass. Do not say that it is only the ordained priest in the sanctuary who offers it, for then you prove that you have never listened to him when he has turned to you with arms extended and cried, "Pray that our sacrifice may become acceptable to God, the Father almighty."

If your imagined friend on Sunday morning were to put his question: "Why are you about so early?" you will have your answer ready: "I am going to offer the Precious Blood once shed on Golgotha. When, at the words of Consecration, the Lord renders Himself present in the Host and in the chalice and thus gives Himself into my hands, then I shall offer Him — He with me, and I with Him — and I shall cry to the Father in Heaven, 'Behold, the Lamb of God, who takes away the sins of the world.' Then, by the Blood of the Covenant, the New and Everlasting Testament from God to men shall be ratified again, and I, a poor sinner, shall be sprinkled again with the Blood that cleanses from all sin. That is why I go to Mass.

"I am going to have my share in an act and deed of my divine Redeemer, my God made man. He and I will have a part in the highest act of worship possible to humanity: a sacrifice of infinite value, a sacrifice worthy of God. Thus I am preparing for the time when I hope I shall stand with the multitude, which no one can number, before God's Throne and the Lamb and sing, 'Benediction, glory, and honor to God and to the Lamb, by whose Blood we were redeemed.' "

Chapter Fifty-Four

☞

Preserve the grace
you received in Baptism

Baptism is a divinely wrought change from death to newness of life. St. Paul loves to repeat that, in Baptism, we have died to the old and risen to the new. As Christ was dead and buried and then rose again, so we also, once dead and buried in sin, have through Baptism risen to the life of grace. Unfortunately, since we were baptized in infancy, we are apt to forget what Baptism has done for us, and the marvel of sanctifying grace is not often realized.

Our Lord's own words that we were born again by water and the Holy Spirit[145] seem only a metaphor to us, not to be taken in too strict a sense. We are all a little like Nicodemus, half-skeptical, and ask how can a man be born again. We take it that nothing much more can be meant than just a change of disposition and outlook, or an external sort of change, being, so to say, at first in God's bad books, and then inscribed in the book of God's favorites. The facts are different.

No change in all the universe is so great as the change that takes place in Baptism. It is veritably a transition from spiritual

[145] John 3:5.

229

death to a divine life. The transformation is so great that it could be brought about only by the creative omnipotence of God. If all the cherubim and seraphim, if all the angelic powers in Heaven worked and labored for ages, they would not be able to give this grace to a single soul; it needs the infinite might of God. Its bestowal is a greater feat of divine power than the "Let there be light" uttered in the beginning of creation. Only God has power over life and death. If this is true of physical life and death, it is still truer of supernatural life and death.

By Baptism we entered into a new world, which by right belongs only to God Himself and to which no created nature, whether of angel or of man, can have access by its own power. We were lifted up beyond the stars of heaven and made fit to dwell in the eternal light that comes from the face of God.

If the baptized child leaves this world in the innocence of his Baptism, he forthwith, in the flash of a moment, will gaze upon God's unveiled countenance and will begin a life of unutterable happiness with his divine Father in Heaven, who in the laver of Baptism made him His adopted child. If the baptized child lives on in this world, his earthly life will be that of a child of God, waiting for his heavenly inheritance and his entrance into his Father's house.

Already here on earth he will be allowed to partake of the Banquet of God in which the Manna that comes from Heaven is given as food in Holy Communion. The Holy Spirit will make him His Temple in which He dwells in Confirmation. The angels of God will guard him, lest he should dash his foot against a stone.[146] The light-bearer, Michael, is ready to take him, when the fullness of his days has come, before the throne of God. If only he has died in the grace of his baptism, he is destined for an endless jubilee of joy with the blessed in glory.

[146] Cf. Ps. 90:11-12 (RSV = Ps. 91:11-12).

So great is Baptism that those who depart this world clad in the white garment of its grace will never again know death, but will live with God forevermore.

The new life bestowed in Baptism is not essentially different from our future life in Heaven. It is related to it as the bud is to the flower, or the seed to the fruit. It is radically the same thing. Heaven is not a sort of external reward, a prize unconnected with our previous earthly life, or a sum of money paid for labor done. It is a development, an unfolding, a grace coming to maturity. Eternal life is given in Baptism. Unless destroyed by sin, it continues in Heaven, the obstacle of death being taken away. Keep the grace of your Baptism, and all will be well for eternity.

Chapter Fifty-Five

☙

Adore the Trinity
in the Blessed Sacrament

Deep in the human heart is the desire to be remembered. Life on earth is short, and human nature craves that, when we shall have gone from this world, people should keep us in mind. It is one of the bitterest thoughts to be utterly forgotten. Jesus, our Lord, although He was God, was also man, and as God made man, when the last day of His mortal life had come, He, too, felt this imperious desire, and he bethought Himself what He would do so that He might be remembered by the children of men. He wished it indeed for His own sake, but He wished it more for their sake, for all their salvation would lie in the remembrance of Him.

Human beings can set up only empty monuments that are mere substitutes for their presence, and, in fact, emphasize their real absence — pyramids and pillars, statues and inscriptions, in brass or marble, telling where once they were and now they are no more — but Christ raised a monument that is the sacrament of His Real Presence, a presence thinly veiled to the eyes of faith by outward appearances of bread and wine.

The Blessed Sacrament is a masterpiece of omnipotence, wisdom, and love. It is a masterpiece of omnipotence, for it needed

233

God's power to change the inner reality of things and yet leave all outward species perceptible to the senses of men, to maintain the semblance of bread and wine and yet to replace the substance within by the real Body and Blood of God's only Son. It is a masterpiece of wisdom, of divine ingenuity, we might say, that Christ's presence might be multiplied a myriad times wheresoever His disciples are gathered together on earth. It is a masterpiece of love, for who but divine Love would have deigned to hide under such lowly appearances as those of this sacrament?

Thus, infinite might and wisdom and love built the unique memorial, which is not an empty shrine, nor a mere resemblance, but the Real Presence of Him who, invisible to bodily eyes, is visible to the eyes of faith as still dwelling in the midst of men. Christ raised to Himself a monument so little to human eyes, so great in divine truth, so insignificant to the senses, so supreme in immeasurable value to the human soul. It contains within itself all Christian mysteries and brings them so close to us that thereby we are made intimate with, and almost take to our bosom, the mystery of God, three in one, the mystery of God incarnate, the mystery of the Atonement, the mystery of the world to come, for the Blessed Sacrament is the pledge of life everlasting.

In the Blessed Sacrament is God the Son, the only begotten of the Father, who was conceived of the Holy Spirit and born of the Virgin Mary. And where one divine Person is, there are all Three; hence, in adoring the Blessed Sacrament, we adore the Son, who reigns with His Father in the Holy Spirit. In adoring the Blessed Sacrament, we worship God in the sacred humanity He has taken; we remember Bethlehem, Nazareth, and Calvary, for He is present who was born on Christmas night, lived a hidden life for thirty years, and died on the Cross of Calvary. In adoring the Blessed Sacrament, we give thanks for our atonement and redemption, for He is there who is ever the Lamb of God who takes away the sins of the world. And in each Mass is mystically offered to God the

Precious Blood, the price of our redemption, which is being shed unto forgiveness of sins.

In adoring the Blessed Sacrament, we strengthen our hope for eternal life, for He is present who promised that if anyone eats of this Bread, He would raise him up on the last day.[147] Thus, the sacred Host is our food of immortality. The Blessed Sacrament says to all who kneel before it, "I am the Resurrection and the Life; he that liveth and believeth in me shall not die forever."[148] Thus, the Blessed Eucharist is the compendium, the all-embracing memorial, of what our Lord did and taught, and of what Christ is even now that He sits in glory at the right hand of God, His Father almighty, while among us He hides His glory under simple sacramental veils.

Let us, then, joyfully praise God, with songs and hymns, glorifying Him who left us so mighty and so tender a memorial of all His marvelous works.

[147] John 6:55 (RSV = John 6:54).
[148] Cf. John 11:25.

Chapter Fifty-Six

Let your confession make you holier

Protestants taunt that Catholics make things easy: they sin, tell the priest about it, and then sin again. If Catholics wished to answer the fool according to his folly, they could retort, "You sin, and tell God about it, to whom it is no news, and then sin again."

Catholics know well enough that without contrition, without real, genuine sorrow, even the priest's absolution is worthless. Their voluntary humiliation in telling a fellowman of their sin is at least some guarantee that their sorrow is genuine. Catholics who go to Confession without any contrition, without any purpose of amendment must be few. A man who is not sorry stays away. But, granted that the absolution is valid and the penitent's sins are forgiven, and his leprosy cleansed, are there not many who resemble the nine lepers in the Gospel who did not return to our Lord to give thanks for their cure?[149]

After Confession, no doubt, we are sincerely happy that the burden of our sin has been removed, and we have made up our minds never to do the horrid thing again. But we are soon out of the church again, perchance even before fulfilling our penance;

[149] Luke 17:12-18.

we are in such a hurry. The round of our daily occupation calls us. Half an hour later, we are immersed in a multitude of distractions, even of pleasures. We may be sitting in a theater, enjoying a movie; we certainly do not have the mien of forgiven penitent sinners. Perhaps that very evening we go to bed certainly without any extra prayers.

For a short time, the sense of relief in having the consciousness of sin off our soul and being no longer in danger of Hell remains with us, but before long all goes on as usual. At most we succeed in keeping away from the kind of sin we confessed. There is no increase in loving devotion to our Lord, no progress in virtue. With no loud voice did we glorify God, nor did we fall on our face before Jesus' feet giving thanks that He had cured us from the leprosy of sin. It was a very humdrum affair; we did the absolute minimum, but nothing more. We were glad when the ordeal was over and then more or less tried to forget all about it.

We are an ungrateful crowd. There is nothing of the grateful Samaritan or of Mary Magdalene about us. She loved much, because much had been forgiven her, said our blessed Lord.[150] Much has been forgiven us, but of how many of us could it be said that in consequence we loved Him much? After every absolution, the priest prays that there may be an *augmentum gratiae*, an "increase of grace." We have been absolved so often that we ought to have increased in grace by leaps and bounds, but we behave as if all that mattered was to get rid of the leprosy of sin. Any increase of spiritual health, any gratitude to the divine Healer, beyond the shortest nod of routine acknowledgment is not our custom.

Considering the many millions of absolutions given each year, we ought at least to be a family of saints and spend our time on Calvary with Mary and John underneath the Cross, and yet we are what we are. In large measure, our mediocrity is due to the fact

[150] Luke 7:47.

that, when in trouble, we do indeed "stand afar off, lift up our voice, and cry, 'Jesus, Master, have mercy on us,' "[151] but when, at Jesus' behest, we have gone to His priests for the hundredth time, we have come away healed, of course, but not in haste to run back and kiss the feet, wounded for our sins, and ask Him what we might do to make up for the past and better please Him, whom we have so much offended.

[151] Luke 17:12-13.

Part Nine

*Keep your gaze
fixed on Heaven*

⌒

Chapter Fifty-Seven

Be confident that the
mighty God protects you

The name of St. Michael forthwith brings to our mind the idea of a battle in Heaven and of a victory won. He is the prince of the heavenly host; he is the warrior of God. The dragon, the old serpent, had swept with his tail a third of the stars of heaven out of the firmament, as the Scripture puts it, but he had found his match in that celestial hero, who rallied the angel sons of God.[152]

Holy Writ gives us mysterious glimpses into the nature and activity of that mighty spirit, who seems to us a lightsome image of God's uncreated majesty. St. Michael's very name contains a revelation of his innermost life, for it is a cry both of wonder and of defiance. It is a cry of wonder, meaning, "Who is like God?" It is a cry of adoring amazement at the unique sovereignty of his divine Creator, the peerless glory by which God in infinite measure transcends whatsoever is made by His hands.

The modern mind has lost the celestial gift of wonder at God and admiration at His glory. The god of those of the modern mind is only a magnified man, a sort of soul of the universe, not

---

[152] Apoc. 12:4, 7-9 (RSV = Rev. 12:4, 7-9).

extending beyond the outermost star. Their word *god* is but a courteous substitute for "nature." They give you the distance of the stars from the earth and want you to be awed by the cyphers and marvel at the number of yards, but the God who spoke, " 'Let there be light,' and there was light,"[153] Him they adore not.

They know not that there are higher mathematics than the highest of theirs in the acknowledgment of our littleness in the presence of the divine majesty, eternal wisdom, and sovereign power from which all things came and have their being.

> *St. Michael,*
> *whose life is one unending cry of amazement,*
> *one paean of praise at the solitary greatness of God,*
> *who alone is enthroned above the cherubim,*
> *obtain for us poor mortals a portion of thy gift.*
> *May we also adoringly say, "Who is like God?"*
> *May we see the smallness and insignificance*
> *of all created things compared with Him, and*
> *in loving humility say, "O God, there is none like Thee.*
> *We gaze and gasp at the thought of Thy greatness*
> *and, prostrate before Thee, we murmur,*
> *'Thou art alone; there is none beside Thee.' "*

Michael's name is also a challenge, a shout of defiance against the foe. If all the power of men and of demons stood against us in battle array, we should still, like Michael, cry, "Who is like God?"

If God is with us, it matters not who is against us. Human nature, if left to itself, might shrink back in terror before the powers of evil, cower and cringe before the might of brute force, but he who dwells in the hidden home of God on high and has found shelter in the shadow of the Almighty, may well say what the psalmist said:

[153] Cf. Gen. 1:3.

"I am safe with Thee; my stronghold is my God, whom I trust. With His shoulders He will overshadow me, and under His wings is a place most secure. I shall not be afraid of the terror by night, nor of the arrow that flieth by day, nor of the treason that moves in the dark and the dusk, nor of the attack of the monster at noon. Though a thousand fall at my side and a myriad at my right hand, unto me it will not come nigh. Since I have set my love on God, God shall deliver me. He shall set me on high, for I have called on His name."[154]

It was this calm confidence in the irresistible might of God that made St. Michael say in his battle with Satan, "May God rebuke thee!" And this divine rebuke made the demon recoil from his evil intent.

We Christians are fully aware that our battle is with foes whose cunning and strength far exceed ours, yet we are not defeatists in the war on the issue of which our eternity depends, for we have our Emmanuel, our God with us, and who is like God?

> *Mighty archangel,*
> *leader of the legions of God,*
> *be thou to each one of us,*
> *even the humblest and the simplest,*
> *an ally, yea, a brother in the*
> *fearsome fight with the powers of darkness*
> *that perpetual light one day may shine upon us*
> *and give us peace everlasting.*

---

[154] Cf. Ps. 90:2, 4-7, 14 (RSV = Ps. 91:2, 4-7, 14).

⌒

Chapter Fifty-Eight

Know that Christ
is always with you

"The Lord Jesus, after He had spoken to them, was taken up into Heaven and sitteth at the right hand of God. But they, going forth, preached everywhere, the Lord working withal and confirming the word with signs that followed."[155] Thus ends the Gospel of St. Mark. St. Paul echoes these words in speaking of "Jesus Christ, who died and is risen again, and who is at the right hand of God, always making intercession for us."[156]

Thus were fulfilled the ancient prophecies: "The Lord saith unto my Lord: Sit Thou at my right hand. . . . The scepter of Thy power the Lord shall stretch forth from Sion; be Thou Lord in the midst of Thy foes. With Thee is the princedom in the day of Thy power among the splendors of the saints. I have been established by Him King over Sion. He said unto me: My Son art Thou; ask and I shall give Thee the gentiles as an inheritance and as Thy possession the ends of the earth."[157]

[155] Mark 16:19-20.
[156] Cf. Rom. 8:34.
[157] Cf. Ps. 109:1-3; 2:6-8 (RSV = Ps. 110:1-2; 2:6-8).

We Christians have ever professed that Jesus sits at the right hand of His Father almighty and that of His kingdom there is no end, as the Creed proclaims. And yet, although Christ is enthroned on the seat of the divine majesty above in the joy and peace of eternity, He is an active priest and prophet and ruler in the Church on earth for which He died.

"The Lord hath sworn and he will not repent: Thou art a priest forever according to the order of Melchisedech."[158] He is ever living, as the Scripture says, to make intercession for us. In His sacred humanity, He stands between God and man, the one Mediator between His Father and us, His brethren, His Father's adopted children. He intercedes for us, showing His Father His blessed five wounds, once the tokens of shame and pain, now marks of love and glory. Christ is the great High Priest of all mankind, who has entered into the holy of holies and there ever pleads for all those whom He has redeemed by His Blood. St. John in his revelation saw the Lamb as it were slain, standing upon the altar before the Great White Throne.[159]

On earth this same sacrificial intercession is perpetually continued in the Mass. At every consecration, Christ becomes present under the appearances of bread and wine, the symbols of His Body and Blood, once separated in His death upon the Cross. In the Mass, He gives Himself into the hands of His priests so that they may offer Him to His Father. Thus, He is the active High Priest ever in function, imploring God's mercy and bounty on all creation until the consummation of the world. Thus, God is keeping His oath that He swore and of which He will never repent: "Thou art a priest forever according to the order of Melchisedech." Christ will still be priest when this present world has passed away, when all sins are forgiven and all the elect are rejoicing before

---

[158] Ps. 109:4 (RSV = Ps. 110:4).
[159] Apoc. 5:6 (RSV = Rev. 5:6).

God's throne, and He will eternally offer their praise to His Father almighty.

Christ is still the great Prophet, for He speaks in His Church until the end of the ages. Not in vain has He said to His Apostles, "Whosoever listens to you, listens to me."[160] The voice of the Catholic Church is verily His voice, coming from the lips of mortal men, but being first issued from the mind of the Incarnate Wisdom and Word of God. " 'Go ye and teach,' said He . . . 'and I shall be with you always.' "[161] St. Mark summed up the truth in the simple sentence: "[He] sitteth at the right hand of God. But they, going forth, preached everywhere, He working withal and confirming the word with signs that followed."

He is still the light of the world, and His Church is the candlestick that shows Him to the world. He is the way, the truth, and the life; no one can come to the Father but by Him.[162] He is the everlasting truth conveying Himself to the minds of men by the inner divine enlightenment of their souls, as well as by the outwardly spoken word and incessant teaching and preaching of His Church. As the voice of a man today speaking into a microphone is made audible by the ether to the uttermost ends of the globe, so Christ has made Himself audible to all children of men by the Church He created and maintains to broadcast His message to His brethren as long as they sojourn in this world.

Christ is still the royal Ruler, the gracious King of all His people. It is He who baptizes and by Baptism admits them into His kingdom. He sends the Holy Spirit on them in Confirmation. He feeds them with His own Body in Holy Communion. He absolves them by the ministry of His priests in the confessional if they truly repent. It is He who marries them when they exchange their vows

---

[160] Cf. Luke 10:16.
[161] Cf. Matt. 28:19-20.
[162] John 14:6.

before the altar. He signs and seals them in their last Anointing and prepares them for Heaven.

He rules them and gives them His commands. He explains His law to them by His bishops, for unto His Apostles and their successors He said as last injunction: "Make them observe whatever I have commanded you."[163] Thus, Christ, who ascended into Heaven, did not leave us orphans, nor did He enter a life of idle repose. He lives forever, acting as priest, prophet, and king. He lives and reigns forevermore.

[163] Matt. 28:20.

⌒

Chapter Fifty-Nine

Receive the help God
sends you through His angels

The angel Gabriel announced unto Mary, and she conceived through the Holy Spirit. Let Gabriel stand before us as representative of all the angels of the Lord, that vast host of our elder brethren who stand on the steps of the throne of the majesty on high, and yet are ministering spirits, sent to minister to us, who shall receive the inheritance of salvation. How cheering, how delightful a revelation of God's bounty that each of us should have our guardian from among the blessed throng of spirit-friends of God, and that the concerns of men are the concerns of angels also.

So close is the interest that the angel world takes in the world of man that Christ told us there was joy in Heaven about one sinner who does penance and that it is dangerous to give scandal to a child, since the child's angel always sees the face of God the Father in Heaven.[164] The Scriptures tell us that even the temporal affairs of men are in the charge of angels. "He has given His angels charge over thee, lest thou dash thy foot against a stone."[165]

[164] Matt. 18:10.
[165] Cf. Ps. 90:11-12 (RSV = Ps. 91:11-12).

An angel moved the waters that cured the sick at Bethesda,[166] an angel kept Tobias safe and cured his father,[167] an angel led Peter out of prison,[168] and thus scores of instances could be cited from the Bible, that even our homely and personal needs are not beyond their care. But, above all, it is the spiritual affairs of men that belong to the sphere of their ministry. Our Christmas was their feast also. They sang in the sky for joy. Our Easter was their feast as well as ours. For very mirth, they shook the earth and made it quake, when they rolled the stone away from the tomb of the risen Christ.

Although they themselves are ever in heavenly bliss, yet even our human sorrows are their concern, for was it not one of them who was privileged to comfort the human soul of Jesus, our divine Brother, when He was sorrowful unto death in the Garden of Gethsemani?[169]

The name of St. Michael is in our minds naturally associated with the mighty defense of the all-holy Church. He is the hero of God, smiting the foes of God's Church in the name of God, as once he smote the rebel angels on the ramparts of Heaven.

The name of St. Gabriel is in our minds naturally associated with the news of the Incarnation which first he brought to Daniel the prophet and in the fullness of time announced to the Virgin Mary. He is the harbinger of good tidings, the messenger of God to all mankind.

Both archangels deal with the great public affairs of God's kingdom.

St. Raphael manifests God to us in a different, more intimate way. He embodies God's tender kindness in the private domestic

[166] John 5:4.
[167] Tob. 5-11.
[168] Acts 12:7.
[169] Luke 22:43.

affairs of men. Simple household matters, the private interest of every family are committed to loving angelic care.

We know St. Raphael's name from the story of an old blind man and his wife and his only son. In their own humble way, they served God. They prayed much, gave what alms they could, did many works of charity to their neighbors, and were anxiously honest, upright, and just. Yet they seemed not to receive much reward on earth.

They become impoverished, and the old man loses his sight. They are in need of the money that, in their kindness, they had lent long ago to a neighbor who had since traveled far away. Someone must go and fetch it, and there is no one to do it but their young son. It is terrible to be deprived of his aid and presence for so many months, but the old couple must face their lonesomeness, for there is no other way out. Their son is but a youth, and the journey is dangerous; they hardly dare send him without a companion. Hoping against hope, they tell him to look for someone who is going the same way.

He is strangely fortunate: he finds someone who has to go to the same place. This someone protects him against all perils, happily assists at his marriage with the daughter of the debtor, brings both safely back to the old folks at home, and miraculously cures the old man of his blindness. They offer him in gratitude half the money of the recovered debt. The mysterious companion smiles and says, "I am Raphael, one of the Seven Angels who always stand before the presence of God. While you prayed and gave alms, it was I who offered your prayers to God. Give unto God the praise."[170] At these words, his gracious figure vanished from their sight. Thus he proved God's affectionate care for little people and little affairs.

God's care is not only for governments and armies, for parliaments or battlefields, for the so-called big matters of races and

[170] Cf. Tob. 12:15, 18.

nations. The wings of God's angels overshadow the humble homes of God's friends whose names are not mentioned in state papers or dispatches.

Mothers and fathers, when your children grow up and they must go far away, commend them to the angels of God. Some of your dear ones may be far away, but this earth is not large for angels, and they are good travelers. They are strong and loving companions for all those entrusted to their care. Be not afraid to invoke them for your children and for yourselves.

Are you in difficulties? Are your household affairs in a bad way? Do people owe you money and have not paid you? Are you steadily getting poorer and poorer? Is your health undermined, or illness upon you that brings disaster to your home? Remember St. Raphael. His name means "Medicine of God"; this means that it is God who heals, God who brings help in desperate cases, when no human remedy is any good.

The story of St. Raphael tells you to what lengths God will go in sending His angels to your assistance in your need, if you are God's servants and pray and are kind and just to your neighbor. Say to yourself, "If God sent St. Raphael to the family of Tobias in the days of the Old Testament before the day when He sent His only-begotten Son on Christmas night, what will God not do for us, who are the brothers and sisters of Jesus, God made man?"

Chapter Sixty

⌒

Believe that good will triumph

Many people are sorely distressed, if not almost scandalized, at the success of Christ's enemies in these days, and the apparent defeat that Christ's cause is suffering in so many lands — in some places, Christians face persecution; in others, the remnants of Christian dogma and morals is dwindling to almost nothing; many either deluded or malignant people openly favor atheism and push cunning propaganda of everything which tends to the destruction of Christianity, of Christian decency and virtue.

"Blessed are those who are not scandalized in me,"[171] Christ said, and we may well imagine that Christ is whispering these words in our ears. God is patient because He is eternal, says a proverb. To us, a period of Church history lasting one whole generation seems very long, but to God, a thousand years are as one day.[172] During the two thousand years of her existence, the Church of Christ has passed through many vicissitudes, and Christ's Church may have still many thousands of years before her ere Jesus Christ comes on the clouds of heaven to judge the living and the dead.

[171] Cf. Matt. 11:6.
[172] Ps. 89:4 (RSV = Ps. 90:4).

...dgment may be during our lifetime, or it may be ten ... years hence; no one can tell. If it should be in our life- ...e ourselves shall see Him in great power and majesty on the ...s of heaven with myriad angels around Him, and the cause of ...rist will be vindicated in the sight of all men. Should Christ's return be a million years hence, we shall likewise be there and share in the triumph of the King of ages, and His delay will seem but a short moment when it is over and gone, for the angel shall proclaim that time shall be no more, and Christ Himself shall say, "Behold I make all things new."[173]

Let us remember, moreover, that even the triumph of evil here on earth is more seeming than real. God's enemies slaughtered many scores of thousands of innocent people because they were devoted to Him. In a sense, it may be sad, yet in another sense, it is very glorious. For when their saintly and sacred victims were dead, what could their persecutors do? When, after agony and shame, these persecuted servants of God breathed their last, who had really triumphed: the persecutors or the persecuted? Must not even persecutors die someday, and is their death, when it comes, to be preferred to the death they inflicted?

But they destroyed thousands of churches and trod the Blessed Sacrament underfoot! In a sense, it is unutterably sad, yet in an-other sense, there is consolation to be found even for that. When Christianity was young and most pleasing to God, Christians wor-shiped in caves and catacombs. To our eyes, churches are beautiful and costly, and their destruction is to be wept over, but in God's sight, the beauty of churches consists mostly in the love of His children, who built them as tokens of their willing sacrifice, and perchance there is more love and self-sacrifice now in those perse-cuted countries than there was before. God's true temple is the heart of man.

[173] Apoc. 21:5 (RSV = Rev. 21:5).

If, in the world's big cities, the churches closed, perhaps Christ found refuge in the hearts of many citizens of those hapless cities. Wicked men profaned His tabernacles and trod Him underfoot, but in secret, many a bosom became a tabernacle of the Sacrament of His love, and He found a sweeter welcome in some hasty Communion in a cellar or an attic by someone who risked life and earthly happiness to be able to receive Him. Diabolical fury may trample on His Sacrament, but Him they cannot hurt, however much they hate Him. His sacred, glorified body is beyond the impotent attacks of human malevolence. But what about the future? "This is the victory which overcometh the world: our faith."[174]

"Be of good cheer, little ones," said our Lord. "I have overcome the world."[175] God has sworn it, and He will not repent: the gates of Hell shall not prevail over His Church.[176] Not a moment's doubt should be allowed to enter our mind, lest our Lord should rebuke us: "O you of little faith, why have you doubted?"[177] Instead of doubt, let there be prayer.

[174] 1 John 5:4.
[175] Cf. John 16:33.
[176] Matt. 16:18.
[177] Cf. Matt. 14:31.

Chapter Sixty-One

Remember that you will die

On Ash Wednesday we are rudely told to remember what most men are doing their best to forget. We are told to remember death. Dust we are, and to dust we shall return. Most of us are like the proverbial ostrich, which hides its silly head in the sand in the hope of not being seen by the pursuer.

It is a silly game, this pretending that there is no death! Were there the slightest chance — even one in a million — of escape by keeping up the pretense, there might be something in it, but since the chance is absolutely nil, what is the good of the pretense?

A man once was discussing with a friend the taking of a certain flat. "Don't," said the friend. "Haven't you noticed that one of the windows overlooks a cemetery? I would rather die than live in a flat like that!"

Surely a silly game, this mawkish attempt at forgetting the obvious and imagining that the undertaker will not know where to dispose of our coffin! Yet many people deliberately choose this fools' paradise and will not be torn away from it even when the clammy hand of death is gripping their shoulders. They say it is gruesome and makes you unhappy. Well, it may be gruesome, but it is certainly wholesome.

Ten Minutes a Day to Heaven

Few people have brought on bodily death by thinking about it, but many people have brought on the death of the soul by forgetting about it. To remember death is to bring to mind the eternal years beyond. To keep the eternal years in mind is to see this life in its true perspective: both its greatness and its littleness. We see its greatness, for in this life alone, and on this side of the grave alone, we are fashioning and forming our life for eternity, since what we make of ourselves here is what we shall be there in the timeless life beyond the tomb.

We see this life's littleness, for "this world passeth away and the fashion thereof."[178] We shall take nothing with us to the grave. The millionaire will then be as poor as the beggar, the nobleman as undistinguished as the commoner, and the scientist will have no further use for his experiments and research. It is the thought of death that makes us say, "Vanity of vanities, and all is vanity,"[179] except to love God and to serve Him alone! To remember death is to recall the dust whence we came and is an aid to destroy within us that persistent pride which is the bane of our existence ever since the Fall.

Since from the slime of the earth we were taken and unto it we shall return, why should we make a song about it or fill the air with our bragging, as the ass fills it with his braying? The thought of death is like a sobering draught to a half-drunken man: it clears the air and blows the haze away, which our befogging self-esteem and the reek of our passions create around us. Many a man has been saved in the moment of almost overwhelming temptation; many a man, even after grievous sin, has been brought to repentance by a reminder of death, or by the sudden sight of a dead face.

Our holy mother, the Church, is not cruel, but kind and wise in calling us up once a year to the stern ceremony of having ashes

---

[178] 1 Cor. 7:31.
[179] Eccles. 1:2.

placed on our forehead and being gruffly reminded of the end of our days here on earth. Society may think it bad form to mention such unpalatable things as death in company, but the Church knows too well that human life is not confined to a drawing-room. Let us, as sensible men and Christians, face the full reality and prepare for it.

The solemnity of Ash Wednesday must be more to us than a routine ceremony. Yes, we shall, all of us, die; where, when, and how we know not, but the fact is beyond cavil and dispute. Although we cannot alter it, we can lovingly accept it from the hands of God.

We may hope that we may die in His grace, that we may die fortified with the sacraments of Penance, Anointing of the Sick, and the most holy Eucharist, that we may gain the plenary indulgence of the last blessing, that our last words may be the holy names of Jesus, Mary, and Joseph, that they may assist us in our last agony, that St. Michael the archangel may carry our soul into the holy light before the throne of God, and that thus we shall be safe for all eternity.

It is worth a lifetime of self-restraint and mortification, a life of prayer and devotion, a life of battle against temptation, thus to depart from this land of exile to our heavenly country, where lies our home with God, our Father in Heaven.

It may be a sharp and painful passage, perhaps, from this life unto the next, but it will be an unspeakable joy to land on the other shore, where God will welcome us and wipe away the tears from our eyes and fill us with the blessed certainty that the fear of death is forever past and life everlasting has begun, the life that knows no end.

Chapter Sixty-Two

Persevere on your journey to Heaven

A youth happened to stand near one of the vigorous mountain streams in the Pyrenees. "Get me a boat," he cried. "My father stays in a village some miles higher up, and I must see him. A boat will be the easiest and quickest way." "But it is upstream, sir," said the boatman. "Ah, what of it!" replied the youth. "I handled an oar ever since I was a little boy. I come from the Broads in Norfolk."

So saying, he jumped into the skiff, and a few powerful strokes soon bore him away. After the first outburst of energy, he thought he would rest on his oars a few minutes to renew his strength, as he used to when rowing in his home country. After less than half a minute, the boat was floating down river with increasing speed. He pluckily grasped the oars again and continued his journey, but before long he felt he must really stop a minute or two and had to let the boat drift back quite a distance.

With grim determination, he plied the oars again. Thus he did a dozen times, and the further he went, the harder it became. He had courage and held out, until, in a bath of sweat, with aching limbs, drooping head, and gasping mouth, he sank exhausted at the feet of his father, who lifted him up and said, "Well done, my son. From where you came to where I am is upstream all the way. It is not like the still, even waters of the Broads. It is several hundred feet above the plain. But you have done it. I am proud of you."

This is a parable. The father is our Father who is in Heaven, and the youth is the plucky Christian who persevered unto the end. We have all heard of the distinction between the natural and the supernatural. The Christian religion is supernatural. The world is satisfied with the natural. The world is on the natural plane, the broad, the wide, easier plane.

Rowing on the world's broads is not so difficult. Be a decent person, don't do anything outrageous against the common standards, fall in with current opinion, don't interfere with your neighbor, live and let live, and you'll drift along fairly pleasantly and smoothly through life, and at death you may even get a quarter of a column of praise in the local paper as an excellent citizen.

God is more exacting. He lives in higher regions. He is not impressed by a newspaper paragraph. One might be an "excellent citizen" and yet a very bad man. We are told to overcome the world, not to glide along upon it.

To overcome the world is uphill work. This is the victory that overcometh the world: our faith.[180] Worldliness is like the pull of gravity on those who want to ride to Heaven. It never ceases acting. The opinion of most of our fellow countrymen is, I am afraid, quite different. They think we get to Heaven by "just going along." Somehow everybody gets there, except possibly great criminals and the monstrously depraved, and even they have it only postponed.

It is all very comfortable, but it happens to be untrue. It is not Christianity. According to Christianity, the way to Heaven is steep, narrow, and hard. It provides no Pullman cars nonstop to

[180] 1 John 5:4.

Brighton, however bright God's heavenly Jerusalem may be. Overcoming the world is no slight task; it can be done only through grace in the strength of faith.

Faith must ever put before our eyes that the ascent to God, however laborious and painful it may be, is worth it, for our Father in Heaven is waiting for us, and His reward is exceedingly great. To raise ourselves above the level of our common humanity cannot be done except by the power of God, and the power of God is at our disposal only if we pray.

Prayers are the oars that propel us toward God, upstream toward His heights. If we cease to pray, we slide back to the mere natural plane of our fallen nature, the stagnant pool of the world. We do not overcome it. It overcomes us. We are swallowed up by the multitude. We take it easy. We do what everybody does. We boast of it even. We are drifting away from God.

⌒

Chapter Sixty-Three

Look to Mary in glory

Although our Lady died, her blessed body did not see corruption, but was assumed by God into Heaven, where, with her divine Son, she is present with both body and soul. Thus, in her case, God anticipated the general resurrection. The early legends about the way Mary's Assumption became known we treat with affectionate interest, but only the great fact itself is part of the Faith of Catholics.

In our Lady's Assumption, then, we celebrate the triumph of humility, the reward for suffering, and the enthronement of purity.

We celebrate the triumph of humility: An unknown workman's wife, the mother of an only Child who died a criminal's death, a woman whose own date and place of death remained unknown to the world, is exalted above all other creatures that ever came from the hands of God.

She gained the supreme victory in the age-long struggle between the Serpent and mankind. She placed her heel upon his head and trod him underfoot.[181] God had looked down upon the lowliness of His handmaid and had done great things in her.[182]

---

[181] Cf. Gen. 3:15.
[182] Cf. Luke 1:48-49.

When, on her feast day, we look up to Heaven and hear her eternal *Magnificat*,[183] we rejoice to think that what was little, lost, and forgotten in the esteem of men was strong and great in the sight of God and achieved a victory that was greater than any ever won in the sorry quarrels of mankind.

Earthly grandeur and worldly power clearly count for nothing in the realm of everlasting values, for God has raised a little maid to be the great Mother of God and the mighty heroine of Heaven. Thus has God shown that the first shall be the last and the last shall be the first.[184]

> *Thou, little maid of Nazareth,*
> *who didst tremble when Gabriel*
> *came to tell thee of God's*
> *tremendous designs concerning thee,*
> *didst bend thy head and say,*
> *"Behold the handmaid of the Lord.*
> *Be it done to me according to thy word."*
> *Thus, in humility thou didst become strong,*
> *and proceeding from strength to strength,*
> *thou didst conquer the kingdom of God,*
> *in the grace of God, and the realm*
> *of thy humble conquest*
> *shall be thine forevermore.*

We celebrate the reward for suffering: "Woman, a sword thy heart shall pierce," said Simeon to the Virgin Mother when she brought her Babe to the Temple.[185] And the prophecy was fulfilled. She became the Mother of Sorrows and the Queen of Martyrs underneath the Cross, where she saw the lifeblood ebb from the

[183] Luke 1:46-55.
[184] Cf. Matt. 19:30.
[185] Luke 2:35.

mangled body of her Son, where she heard Him utter His great cry and give up the ghost, where they laid the lifeless form of her Son in her lap, tormented and done to death by the children of men.

She had stood on Calvary and borne the pain, and then she had lived through years of lonesome sorrow until at last came to her also the end of days. But God never causes suffering only for suffering's sake. God allows suffering in order that He may make up for it and reward it with the riches of His bounty. The Queen of Sorrow had to become the Queen of Holy Joy.

Not only does God dry the tears from the eyes of His saints, but it stands written that He makes all things new. Christ, with the glorified wounds from the nails and from the spear still on His sacred body, met His dear Mother and caused her tears to change into heavenly smiles, and He made her happier than He made the widow of Naim, to whom He said, "Woman, cry no more," and gave her back her son.[186]

"Mother, behold I make all things new. The cry and the clamor of Calvary is over. The lonesomeness of life without me is past. The sky shall never darken again in the eternal light of happiness. For pain, I give thee pleasure, for sorrow, exultation, that thou shouldst sing thy *Magnificat* forevermore. Thou hast suffered much, my Mother, but I repay!"

We celebrate the enthronement of purity. After the first Eve's fall, it seemed for a long while as if no unstained human creature should occupy the throne destined for someone who had never sinned. True, fallen man had repented, but it was always fallen man. And was no human person ever to be enthroned in the spotlessness of untouched human nature? Was no second Eve ever to sit near the throne of the second Adam, God made man, in Heaven, and thus the Fall in Paradise be utterly undone? Should the bodies of all be given to the corruption of the grave in

---

[186] Cf. Luke 7:13-15.

consequence of sin, and none pass from earth straight to Heaven in body and soul, because for a while they had been the children of wrath?

God happily decided otherwise. Our faith in our Lady's Assumption tells us that a sinless body should not molder in the tomb, that what had never known the taint of sin should not know the worm of the grave. In the radiance of her innocence, the white splendor of her untarnished glory, God eagerly took her as the greatest prize of His Redemption, as one so completely redeemed that for her it would eternally be as if the Fall had never been and sin had never reigned.

We banished children of Eve look up from this vale of tears to the throne of the second Eve, our spiritual mother, rejoicing at the glorification of her body and the exaltation of her soul, and beg her to continue her *Magnificat* for herself and for us, for by her intercession we hope to be one day where she is and glorify God, who brought redemption to men.

Chapter Sixty-Four

Contemplate Heaven

"We wait for the adoption of the sons of God: the redemption of our body":[187] when we get to Heaven, our soul will be flooded with happiness in the sight of God. Seeing God face-to-face is the essence of our celestial bliss, but after the general resurrection, our body also shall have its share. Only then shall our adoption be fully consummated, when the glory and joy of our soul shall abound and flow over into the whole of our human nature. We shall be, not disembodied spirits, but men and women again, radiant in the glory of God as a crystal is transparent in the light of the sun.

Of that celestial, yet truly human, life, it is difficult to form an adequate idea, for of that is the word of Scripture true, that as yet "No eye hath ever seen, no ear hath ever heard, neither hath it entered into the heart of man what God hath prepared for those that love him."[188] Reason and revelation, however, have not left us completely without help in picturing the delights of our risen life.

We know that the children of the resurrection, as Christ calls the blessed, shall neither marry nor be given in marriage, for they

[187] Cf. Rom. 8:23.
[188] 1 Cor. 2:9.

shall be like the angels in Heaven.[189] They shall neither hunger nor thirst, yet in some mysterious way, they shall be sated with the plenty of God's house, and God shall give them to drink of the torrent of divine joy, for He is the fountain of life. They shall not cry, nor mourn forevermore, for God has wiped away the tears from the eyes of His saints, as it stands written in the word of God.[190] They shall have put on immortality and be clothed in incorruption; the ills and aches of mortal flesh they shall never know again. The dread of old age and of death shall have gone, since they will have entered into life everlasting.

Death lies behind them, and before them lies eternal youth. The light eternal shines in their eyes, for they shall be always young. Rest eternal has come to them after the hard tasks of earthly life, and the curse of a life in the sweat of their brow has been lifted. It shall be rest, yet measureless energy without fatigue, unabated vigor without weariness. All the universe shall lie open to their delighted gaze, and no corner of God's wide world shall lie inaccessible to them. Their glorified bodies shall indeed remain truly physical and material, even as the body of the risen Christ which the Apostles touched and which St. Thomas was allowed to feel and handle, yet for all that, their bodies shall be spirit-like and endowed with powers, now unknown to sluggish human nature.

They shall move with the ease and swiftness of light. Nothing shall hinder them, for they shall pass, if need be, through solid rock, even as Christ did on Easter morn. A sheen of glory shall accompany them, and the majesty of their gait shall be the admiration of angels, for the angel world shall pay them homage because they are the brothers and sisters of Jesus Christ, who is the King of both angels and men. With the angels, they shall make one

---

[189] Luke 20:36.

[190] Apoc. 21:4 (RSV = Rev. 21:4).

loving, merry company of creatures who are the adopted children of God, the Father almighty.

Among themselves, the multitude of the blessed shall make one human, glorified family. However vast God's eternal household will be, affectionate exchanges shall reign between all the members thereof. The intimacies of human life will be a thousand times sweeter in Heaven than they can ever be on earth. The mother shall love her son and the fond father his daughter, and brother shall embrace brother, sister shall kiss sister.

Glorified nature is nature still, and the charm of manhood and womanhood will not be lessened; rather, it will be spiritualized and hallowed in God-given sanctity. The great saints whose names we now mention with awe shall be our familiar friends. The homeliness of Heaven shall encompass the highest and the lowest, for God's house is not a cold palace, nor are His children drilled like stiff, unbending courtiers.

What precise merriment, what amusing entrancement will be provided during the never-ending feast day of Heaven we cannot conceive, let alone describe.

But since we shall have human bodily eyes wherewith to see, scenes of beauty must unroll themselves before our gaze without ever wearying our sight. Since we shall have human bodily ears to hear, melodies soft and mighty, music tender and absorbing shall throw us into ecstasy. Since we shall have lips to speak, they shall move in the language of the blessed, more wonderfully than the lips of the Apostles on Pentecost day. Since eternally our throat is made for song, we shall sing God's praises, now in solitary bursts of awe and joy, then in the harmony of a thousand choirs. We shall find gladness in the odor and freshness of a springtide that will never be spoiled by summer heat or winter frost.

Indeed, no eye has ever seen, nor as yet has ear ever heard, nor has it entered into the heart of man what God has prepared for those who love Him.

⌒

J. P. Arendzen
(1873-1954)

John Peter Arendzen studied with the Christian Brothers in his native Amsterdam and later at Hageveld College in Leyden, at St. Thomas's Seminary in Hammersmith, London, at the Universities of Bonn and Munich, and at Christ's College in Cambridge, England. He was ordained a priest in 1895.

During his studies at Cambridge, he was assigned to St. Ive's parish as a member of the Catholic Missionary Society, founded by Cardinal Vaughan in 1902. The society was composed of priests who were willing "to spend their lives as itinerant missionaries in Neo-Pagan England and preach the Catholic Faith to those who had almost forgotten what the word meant."[191] Fr. Arendzen taught at St. Edmund's College in Ware until 1949 and spent his remaining years in Kilburn, North London.

The eloquence and clarity that earned him a place in the *Daily Mail's* "Preachers of the Century" is reflected in his writings, which include books, such as *Prophets, Priests, and Publicans* and

---

[191] J. P. Arendzen, "Five and Twenty Years," *Catholic Gazette*, March 1927.

Ten Minutes a Day to Heaven

Purgatory and Heaven, essays, annotations in the Douay Bible, and entries in the *Catholic Encyclopedia.* Fr. Arendzen's strong, clear explanations of the Faith challenge, equip, and motivate today's readers to continue his missionary work of spreading the gospel in our increasingly secular world.